A Crash Course
in Starting a Business

A Crash Course
in Starting a Business

Scott L. Girard, Jr., Michael F. O'Keefe & Marc A. Price

The Crash Course Series

Series Editor: Scott L. Girard, Jr.

To Gaye, Lynda, Marci & Stef.

Acknowledgments

Scott wishes to thank: His wife - Kellin, his co-authors, his parents, the Girard Family, the Conway Family, the Edwards Family, the Seaman Family, the Warren Family (keep up the writing, Lea), the O'Keefe Family, everyone at Pinpoint Holdings Group, Barbara Stephens, Jack Chambless, Mary-Jo Tracy, Sandra McMonagle, Diane Orsini, Nathan Holic, Peter Telep, Pat Rushin, the Seminole Battalion, Dawn Price, and the Republic of Colombia (for the sweet, sweet brown nectar by which this project was fueled).

Mike wishes to thank: His parents - Tim & Gaye O'Keefe, his co-authors, Jamie, Kimberly Rupert, the O'Keefe Family, the Goldsberry Family, the Roy Family, the soon-to-be Hubert Family, the Murat Family, the Grant Family, the Girard Family, the Price Family, the Holycross Family, the most inspiring professor - Jack Chambless, his two favorite authors - Clive Cussler and Timothy Ferriss, and those individuals in Argentina (for making sure there is always Malbec on the table).

Marc wishes to thank: His wife - Dawn, his co-authors, his mom - Lynda, the Price Family, the O'Bryan Family, the Smith Family, Jean Hughes, Kellin Girard, Mike Schiano, and Howard Satin (his life-long mentor).

The authors would collectively like to thank: Everyone at Expert Business Advice, the Van Beekum Family - Dave, Melissa and the sugar gliders, and Jon Collier.

Preface

I REMEMBER THE EXACT MOMENT that I fully understood what our series of books should accomplish. At that point in time, Mike, Marc and I had only conceptualized that we wanted to write a series for laypersons and people only moderately familiar with entrepreneurship and business. Multitudes of books exist on basic levels (and beyond) of business practices and procedures and all we really knew, moving forward, was that writing another one of *those* books wouldn't really serve anyone or change anything, no matter how well written it was.

On the morning that I "got it," I was drinking coffee and reading the news; the television was on in the background. I glanced up at the television at some point and saw a commercial for one of those foreign language software programs where, in order to teach a language, instead of teaching simply repetitious vocabulary, they culturally immerse the student in the subject by holistically surrounding them with concepts of all manner of things applicable to the subject. In short, they don't list facts and terms and call it teaching—they show the student a vast array of information, on a multitude of levels, thus allowing them to bathe in knowledge.

I knew then that instead of illustrating a bunch of facts that we thought you should know about business, we should take a more holistic approach and help you become conversational in the *language* of business. Our method is most effective if the book is read cover to cover, with nothing left out. If you reach a chapter and think you know everything there is to know about the subject, read it anyway. It'll only take a minute—that's why the chapters are not lengthy. Instead of calling the important information, "important," in the text, you'll know it's important because you'll see it more than once.

If you're looking to read a business book and immediately be the world's greatest businessperson, this book isn't for you. If your goal, however, is to become knowledgeable to a "conversational" level on the broad topic address by this book as a first stepping-stone to greatness, we believe that our book has no rival.

It is my sincere desire that this book not only increase your understanding of the subject, but that it also evoke enjoyment through learning the language of business and to all related aspects of your life.

- Scott

WHEN WE SAT DOWN and decided to engage in the daunting task of writing a series of books for entrepreneurs and small business owners, I cringed. I thought, *how can we ever reduce our advice and experiences to writing, let alone cover enough detail to fill the pages of an entire book?*

Either way, we decided to get started; so each of us began drafting articles that had topics reflective of our specialties and past work experience. Only as the initiative continued did I discover a certain passion for sharing my advice in the first-person point of view, and by trying to convey through words the way it felt to go places, negotiate situations, and experience different things, both good and bad.

So, I hope that the book as a whole can capture your interest, provide valuable information, and share an interesting perspective into the world of entrepreneurship and small business conception.

- Mike

EVERYONE HAS HEARD the phrase *"Knowledge is Power"* at some point in their life. These words are rather simple, yet profound, at the same time. And yet, if ever asked to amend this powerful adage to represent my characterization of this timeless expression, I would probably have it read *"Information is Power"* for a couple of reasons.

Today, we exist in an age of instant information in every facet of our lives. At any given moment, we can receive instant news, on-demand weather and traffic reports, sports scores, social media happenings, and stock market updates, to name only a few. And yet, much of this information is forgotten within moments of receiving it, as new reports and updates are constantly replacing the data we were just beginning to process.

Most generic information travels fast to keep pace with the demands of our constantly-changing society. On the other hand, some information is meant to stay with us for awhile, if not forever. And with that, Scott, Mike and I set out to write a series of books to reflect those needs.

Our passion for success in business and in life can be felt when reading these pages. And as lifelong, serial entrepreneurs, we have always taken the approach of surrounding ourselves with information, ideas and viewpoints from countless sources to support our efforts in constructing our next project. That information, when reliable and trustworthy enough, can, and will, be used over and over again for repeated success. So, in essence, one could simply profess that information *is* knowledge, if applied over time.

Our series of books represent the hard work, research and application of numerous business philosophies, ideas and viewpoints. And yet, nothing in these pages is truly ground-breaking. You will be hard-pressed to find any earth-shattering techniques, but what you will find is rock-solid information that can be applied now…and later. It's information that can be shared, and then referred to as a refresher down the road, if needed. Our goal here was to compile information that is relevant, smart and timely. It would be our hope you can find success in these fresh and contemporary approaches to the fundamentals of business to get you, and keep you, at the top of your game.

The way forward begins here…

- Marc

Contents

* * *

Part I

Planning

Chapter 1

Entrepreneur: Do You Have What It Takes?

In an economy when so many fail, do you have what it takes to succeed?

* * *

I LIKE TO THINK that somewhere deep inside of everyone, there is an entrepreneur. Humans have survived millions of years when so many other species haven't. We are an intelligent and adaptable group of fighters and survivors. While I believe that anyone can be a successful entrepreneur if they truly want to, it's the "want" that people so often confuse with "can't." The truth is that you really can, but not without sacrifices. At the end of the day, most people aren't willing to dig in and fight the long hard battle to realize success.

Some say that starting a business in today's economy is harder than it's ever been. Some say otherwise. The facts are clear that the resources are plentiful to help a hopeful entrepreneur become successful. The market, however, is so saturated that getting a piece of those resources only comes to those that are willing to fight for it.

The first step is looking inside yourself and deciding if you are the type of person that exudes the most common traits of successful entrepreneurs. There are millions of books in existence written by the brightest minds in business. Do you understand them? Can you relate to them? Have you even heard of them? Any bookstore or library has a vast business section; I recommend that you check it out and pay close attention to the ones who made it big in the area or field that you're considering launching a new business into.

Are you motivated to get things done? Do you act before someone has to tell you to get going? These are very important traits of an entrepreneur because you're the one at the helm. Not only do you have to be comfortable motivating yourself, but also motivating others. You're the boss now, so get used to it.

Are you easily intimidated? Do you tend to avoid competition? If so, you may want to reconsider starting a business. Intimidation and competition will fly at you from all directions and in all different forms. Other businesses, time, paperwork, changing conditions, money—they are all adversaries in your new endeavor and will all play a role in trying to make you fail.

As from the books and other business leaders, part of being a good leader is being a good listener. We weren't born knowing everything so part of being a successful entrepreneur is being able to listen and take advice from others. Quite frankly, you'd be foolish not to.

Finally, take an honest look at yourself. Having a solid understanding of your own strengths and weaknesses is probably the most important part of your pre-execution self-evaluation. When things get tough (believe me that they will, at some point), you have to have the will-power and self-discipline to overcome, as well as the ability to assess risk and make decisions quickly in order to mitigate that risk.

The bottom line here is that not everyone will start and run a business. Not because they *can't*, per se, but because they *won't*. They're not willing to give it their all. The scariest part of it is that people who tell themselves that they will not give up, no matter what, sometimes end up giving up anyway because the struggles they face down the line are greater than they ever imagined.

Keep these final thoughts in mind: starting a business is harder than you think it will be, but it's not impossible. Your mistakes are not failures—they're lessons; learn from them and move on. People all over the world start successful businesses every single day. Are they better than you? Absolutely not! You have what it takes to be successful somewhere inside you; now reach down deep and don't let go until you've arrived where you want to be.

* * *

Chapter 2

What Kind of Business is Best for You?

Every entrepreneur's first question is seldom the easiest. Here are some tips to help you decide and get you pointed in the right direction.

* * *

HERE'S A TRUE STORY. For the first three years of college, I was an international business / economics double-major. I was setting myself up to be a major player in the global business scene. My grades were stellar and it was looking good that I'd land a great job right out of school. I had done extremely well in my summer internships and had proven myself to many leaders in the business circles I had ventured into. There was one problem. Over the years, I had grown to loathe international business. Although I was still excelling, it was a matter of principle, not passion. In short, I grew to learn that international business was *not* the best choice for me to continue to pursue, especially if I wanted to go into business for myself and start my own business.

Answering this question requires one thing: honesty. Do you really want to be an investment banker? Lawyer? Doctor? Or do you really want to be an art director, product designer, race car driver, whatever? Look inside yourself and decide what you would really *love* to do for a living. I'm not going to lie to you and say that that's all you have to do—'if you can dream it, you can do it' kind of boloney. But seriously, deciding what you truly want to do is the first step to starting the right business for you.

If you're in a position like so many others and you really don't know what you love to do (it sounds silly on paper, but it's an extremely common problem for would-be entrepreneurs), think back through your memory about what you're good at as people (usually) like to do what they're good at. What did you achieve awards for growing up? What were your hobbies? On what do you receive compliments from others? If someone on the street stopped you and said, "Listen, I'm a billionaire and I want to bankroll whatever business you want and I'll pay you a million dollars a year to do it," what would you say? What kind of business would you choose to start?

As I stated earlier that it's not quite as simple as "dreaming and doing," the next step, of course, is to conduct research or rational brainstorming about if your dream is plausible or even possible. For instance, if you're fifty years old, I'm sorry, you're not going to be rookie of the year in the NBA. If you want to open a surf shop but live in Lawton, Oklahoma, I don't believe you'll be selling many surfboards there. Market testing is a very important aspect of deciding what kind of business is best for you.

So what happened in my story? I changed my major at the beginning of my senior year and although I was still able to minor in international business and economics, my major was in my true passion: writing. Although it was scary at first, I now know that I made the right choice, despite the risks, because I'm making a very good living doing what I love to do. I will always have my knowledge and insight into the global business and economic arenas, but I now use my passion and talents in my own business to write what I know and convey my knowledge to others on my terms, and in my own voice. My father always said that if you love what you do, you'll never work a day in your life. You know what? He was right.

* * *

Chapter 3

5 Boxes to Check Before Starting a Business

You're not just a soon-to-be entrepreneur; you're also a person with a life. Don't screw it up by jumping the gun on your new business.

* * *

PEOPLE GET SO EXCITED when they feel like they've connected all of the intellectual dots and now have a complete idea to get their new business off the ground. Maybe they finally figured out the chemical composition of their new product, or finally just thought of the perfect name for their business.

Whatever the last piece of the puzzle was, don't let it excite you to the point where you get tunnel vision and run right off of a cliff. Before you go quitting your day job to start your new business, you need to ensure that you check these 5 boxes so that you don't end up right back at your old desk, labeled as a failure.

1. Do you have enough money? It might sound silly, but sometimes people get so wrapped around the axel thinking about money for their new business that they forget to think about other important expenses that they will still be expected to pay like rent, a mortgage, food, car, insurance, etc. Do you have enough money to live on while you're getting your business started? Experts say that by having six months of living expenses saved up is a safe estimate. Just make sure that you're not calling your living expenses "start-up capital," or vice-versa.

2.   Have you conducted a market test? Just because an idea is awesome doesn't mean that it's awesome for where you're starting a business. Snow shoe companies don't do well in Florida, electronics stores don't do well in Amish Pennsylvania, and I don't believe that a Dollar General in Beverly Hills would have a single customer. The reasons why certain establishments don't survive in certain markets are countless. Sometimes, people find out the hard way by going out of business. Research other businesses like yours in the area in which you want to open and see how they're doing.

3.   Did you write a business and/or marketing plan? Do you have any kind of plan at all? If so, is it good enough? Have you covered all of your bases? While part of writing a plan is organization, the other major part is uncovering hidden issues or things you may not have thought of.

4.   Test the water before you dive in. While you still have your day job, try doing as much as you can toward your new endeavor at night. This ties directly to number 2 in that you may be able to conduct a full market test through working at night and on the weekends while you still have your day job. If you can manage this for just a little while, it's a great way to maintain your life's security while testing whether or not your new endeavor will work.

5.   Plan the transition. Brainstorming the strategy of your transition from employee to entrepreneur should be a multi-draft plan. No one, no matter how smart, can effectively plan the transition in one try. There are simply too many facets, including the ones that you can't learn from books and that may be specific and unique to your personal life, to keep track and on top of to plan it all at once. The biggest holistic facet to stay on top of and ensure that you've planned inside and out is your finances.

This can be daunting because not only do you have to consider your new business finances, but your personal finances need to be considered, too. Consider, also, that, typically, things never go as planned. You need to have contingency plans in place for your life-vitals like health, vehicle and home-owners insurance, child care, your mortgage, etc.

It's important to stay on top of your personal finances during the transitional period from employee to entrepreneur because, while no one wants to think about it, in case your endeavor doesn't make it, you don't want to have to look for a new job while trying to put your personal life back together, too.

* * *

Chapter 4

I've Got a Great Idea!
So, Now What?

What to do with great business and product ideas.

* * *

IT'S A PROBLEM no one ever expects to have. Everyone that sits around trying to think of a good business or product idea never considers what to do once they have one. When the light bulb comes on, inventors and soon-to-be entrepreneurs get the look of sheer excitement because they're sure that they've finally thought of the idea that will make them millions. Soon, however, they realize that, while they have a great idea, what they don't have is a plan or task list to get their product launched or their business idea to the next level. Oftentimes, they don't even know what the "next level" is. If you've been in this boat, don't be discouraged; most people are, or have been at one point.

Depending on if you're building your new business on a tangible product idea or an intellectual property idea, the second step (after thinking of the idea) is to protect it with a patent, trademark, copyright, or any combination of two or all three. The United States Patent and Trademark Office website will give you all the information and services you need to protect your product/idea. Once your idea is protected, you can get started planning and acquiring financing.

Not everyone with a great idea, however, wants to start a business. Writers don't write books because they want to start a publishing company, after all. Many people, after coming up with a great idea, want to put it on the open market, sell it, come up with another great idea, and repeat the entire process all over again. It can be tricky selling something on the open market, especially to large corporations. They have entire staffs of people whose jobs it is to write the best contracts or negotiate the best deals on behalf of the company so that, above all else, the company comes out on top.

As such, after making contact with the corporation, secure a fully executed non-disclosure agreement from them. The point of contact for this should be a duly authorized officer who can bind the company to the terms and conditions of your non-disclosure and acknowledge the presence of your copyright protection. It is recommended that you secure this acknowledgement with two steps: the executed non-disclosure agreement, and a signature of acceptance on a letter you draft that requests their acknowledgment of certain specific points (e.g. copyright) that are important to you.

If/when they accept your terms, they will ask you to sign a contract. Although you may think you understand the terms stated in the contract, you would be wise to have legal representation of your own look it over before you sign it.

Once the legalities are taken care of, the hard part is generally over. The biggest point to take away from this is that, although you might be very excited about your new great idea, the safety and security of that great idea should be at the front of your mind.

* * *

Chapter 5

Choosing the Best Type of Business

When conceptualizing a new venture, this decision is seldom given the thought and consideration it deserves. Start your business the right way by addressing this first.

* * *

WHETHER SETTING UP your business as a sole proprietorship, partnership, limited liability company (LLC), S-Corporation, or C-Corporation, it is vital to understand, not only the filing and paperwork requirements, but also the different tax implications that are present with each type of business structure.

Commonly, owner-operated small businesses are set up as sole proprietorships due to the simplicity of the filings and regulation, as well as the single-layer tax impact on the revenues of the business. This type of ownership also allows the owner to be his or her own boss. However, owners should be extremely cautious when dealing as a sole proprietor or in a general partnership.

These two types of business structures allow for all of the liabilities of the business to be shared with the individual owners on a personal level. As such, unlimited liability can be scary. Just remember to hope for the best but plan for the worst. Don't choose a business structure based on the ease and convenience of setting it up. It is more common than one would think to have business situations end in lawsuits resulting in general partners and sole proprietors being sued personally and losing homes, cars and savings accounts. There are plenty of hurtles that these types of business owners have to overcome. Management can be difficult with limited participants and there is commonly a very overwhelming time commitment associated with this type of business.

There are two types of members in a partnership—a general partner and a limited partner. General partners have unlimited liability and are typically managers of the company. Limited partners have exactly what you would think—limited liability, and they usually do not have a role managing the company. Just remember, no matter how well the individual partners get along, one of the most common issues with partnerships is the disagreements that arise between members. This sometimes leads to unfortunate falling-outs between friends.

Most successful types of businesses are corporations—either limited liability companies, conventional corporations (C-Corps), or S-Corporations. These three forms of business ownership comprise approximately 80% of all sales in the United States and they all share two major benefits; the first being that they have limited liability, and the second, they usually qualify for special tax advantages that other types of business ownerships do not. Incorporating a business is a great strategy as it allows for the company to grow, it has perpetual life, ownership can change hands easily, and it's common for corporations to be able to afford talented employees. However, as a sword can cut both ways, there are some disadvantages to incorporating a business. Corporations are more costly to start, they require more paperwork, possible conflicts with other owners and board members can arise, and they are also affected by double taxation, which means that the business' profits will be taxed, as well as the shareholders' dividends.

A special type of incorporation is called and S-Corporation. Aside from sharing the benefit of limited liability, this type of corporation has a major difference from a conventional C-Corporation. It has much simpler taxes, called 'single taxation,' that are similar to that of a partnership. Downsides of incorporating as an S-Corporation include ineligibility for a dividends received deduction, and that S-Corps are not subject to the 10% of taxable income limitation that are applicable to charitable contribution deductions.

Choosing the best type of business is a personal choice, albeit one that shouldn't be taken lightly. The prospected longevity, growth and future development of the business should be taken into serious consideration before the choice to incorporate is made.

* * *

Chapter 6

Do I Need a Business License for My Home Business?

Tips for getting the paperwork aspect out of the way so you can get on to making money at home!

* * *

DEPENDING ON THE TYPE of business you are starting, you may be required to obtain local, county, State or Federal licensing. Since heavy fines are usually associated with conducting a business without proper licenses and permits, it is important to determine which license will be required before you start conducting business.

In general, most small and home-based businesses will only require a local business license or permit. It's important to conduct research and get positive answers, however, because to be held up by red tape or fees when you're trying to launch a new business is the last thing you want.

The good news is that determining what your local licensing requirements are is a simple process. Simply call or visit your city or county government offices (typically in the courthouse) for information about business licensing requirements. Nearly all businesses will require a county or city license to operate. The license is easy to obtain and normally only requires a short visit to the local courthouse. Fees, if any, are small. The exception to this rule is a liquor license. Liquor licenses can be very expensive (over $100,000) and the penalties and fees for serving alcohol without a license can cost more than the license itself and have incarceration rolled up with it. In short, don't serve alcohol without a license; it's not worth it. Enough said.

If you intend to start a home-based business, ensure that, aside from acquiring a business license, you check local zoning requirements (this can typically also be accomplished at the courthouse) as well as any property covenants. Zoning requirements regulate how property can be used and in some cases, some activities may not be allowed in your area.

Some businesses may also require a State license. Examples include attorneys, barbers, contractors, dentists, most businesses serving food, and social workers. Each State has an agency dealing with these types of businesses. You can determine if your business requires a State license by contacting your local government offices. They should be able to give you information as to whether your business will require State licensing. In some cases, these licenses can be expensive.

For a very few businesses, Federal licensing is required. Examples would be a business that is engaged in providing investment advice or dealing with firearms. In general, Federal licensing is required if the business is highly regulated by the government. It is best to consult an attorney in these cases.

Each State has different business licensing requirements. A good source of State specific information is the Internet, specifically your local, county, State, or federal government websites. Not only will they provide answers to all the questions you might have, they will have contact information and downloadable documents with tutorials so that you can begin the process immediately at home. In most cases, you will only have to show up and sign the document. It's even possible, in some cases, that you can complete the entire process at home via the Internet or U.S Mail.

* * *

Chapter 7

How to Create a New Business or Product Name

Just when you thought naming children was hard! Your business or product's name should be smart <u>and</u> functional.

* * *

WHILE THIS SEEMS like a tiny detail, it's actually very important. "Just give it a name and sell it," some people say. And while they're assertiveness is admirable, the name of your new business or product deserves a bit more thought than that. Sometimes, your first instinct is the best one, and other times, it can take days, weeks, or longer to really settle on the perfect name.

There are just as many ways to come up with a good name as there are reasons why you need one. For marketing, it's vital, but also because a good name will draw people to the product or company and thus, the product will be more likely to sell itself. That way, the company will have to spend less on publicity.

We all know when we see a good business or product name. There are several patterns that have evolved over time in the industry. While some people see alliteration (two or more words that start with the same sounding letter) as kitsch, others see it as clever, e.g. Coca-Cola, Kandy Kitchen, Best Buy, Dunkin' Donuts, etc. Same goes for business or product names that consist of two or more words that rhyme. I would say that the general intent of a business or product name is to describe the product or company while being memorable and desirable to the person who reads/views it.

So, where do I start?

Think about your new business or product and decide what message you want to send through it. If want to open a boxing gym, would you even consider naming it, "Sissy Mary's Boxing Gym"? Of course not, you would want something tough-sounding like "Hard Knockers" or "Lights Out Boxing Center". Continuing down that road, what do you know about your industry and the people who patronize it? If you're trying to start something new, chances are, you probably already know quite a bit. Use that knowledge and be creative.

Sometimes, less is more. There is a barbershop in my area called "Tim's Gentlemen's Haircuts," and the place is wildly popular. Tim is the owner and he cuts hair. Enough said. Depending on your product or business, this could work well for you. Sometimes, certain clientele respond better to the direct approach.

Where did the nature of your product or business originate? Sometimes, searching out the nature of your product or business' history can open up a lot of wonderful name ideas. Did the concept begin in a foreign country? While writing a business plan for a friend of mine a few years ago for an imported wine, cheese and meat shop and café that he wanted to open, I suggested that he consider "Le Vie Bien" for the name of the shop. Translated into, "The Good Life," it worked on multiple levels because his products fit the language, the words fit the area (and how consuming his products make you feel). The location was in a quiet, but upscale, part of town so naming the shop Le Vie Bien fit perfectly.

Sometimes people ask me what the most clever and holistically-best business name I've ever seen is. I have to say, while there are many very brilliant business names out there, my very favorite is a tiny, independently-owned mechanic shop near my house named, "Honest Engine Mechanic Shop." Their logo is a smiling Native American holding a wrench in one hand and waving with the other. Brilliant.

The bottom line here is that while thinking of a name for a new product or business is very important, it should also be fun. Don't rush it, but if after a while if you still can't think of anything, there are business and product naming software options and consultants that can assist you.

* * *

Chapter 8

The Difference Between Partners & Investors

Depending on your desired level of someone else's involvement in your company, this choice is one of the most important.

* * *

WHEN YOU ARE looking for financing for your business, understanding the difference between partners and investors is very important. The two parties can help you raise the necessary funds that you need to start and operate your business. However, they both play very different roles in the business.

An investor will basically put money in the business in hopes getting some returns on his/her investment. On the other hand, business partners co-own a business. They raise the capital for the business as per agreement with each other. This explanation of business activity is probably the biggest difference between partners and investors. Business partners share losses and profits while investors expect returns on their investment. The business owner will shoulder the losses and ensure that the investors get good returns on their investment.

Another major difference between partners and investors is in the running of the business. Normally, investors will not participate in the day-to-day running of the business. However, you need to keep them informed of everything; in particular, the accounts of the company. They will want to know how you are spending their money, how the business is performing, and the returns accrued or expected. On the other hand, your business partner has to be involved in all the business operations. You may each play different roles, but you have to both be involved in the decision making.

General partnerships mean that all the business partners share all the business responsibilities equally. For instance, this means that profits and losses are equally shared among all of them. If the business experiences any major problems, all partners will have to accept liability. That means that if they fail to pay taxes and are arrested, all of them will be answerable. With that said, if four partners own a business together, they do not all have to own an equal share. One partner can own 50% himself, while the others only own 50% between the three of them. However, from a responsibility standpoint, when it comes to the investors, they have no obligations to share any responsibilities with the business owners. The difference between partners and investors is that the former is responsible for the business while the later is not.

The liability of the partners may be limited when it comes to limited partnerships (LLC's). However, there is still one partner who has to accept unlimited liability for the company.

In some cases, investors may also be partners. For instance, an angel investor may ask for a share of the company instead of asking for returns on their investment. This is normally based on how he perceives the business' potential and also his own interest in the business. The difference between partners and investors is that while one party assumes immediate co-ownership of the business, the other can decide not to co-own the business at all.

Understanding the difference between partners and investors is important, especially when you need to know where you can get your financing. Both parties can be very helpful to a business, but you need to carry out adequate research in order to decide whether to get financing from partners or investors.

* * *

Chapter 9

How to Write a Business Plan

(The short version)

The best way to take on this large and important project is to learn the basics. Look no further.

* * *

The INTRODUCTION portion of the business plan needs to be a summarized description of the company and its industry of participation. Include any industry standards and statistics that may enhance the appearance of the proposal. In the thesis of the paragraph, clearly state the total capital requirements requested of the reader (investor, bank, etc.).

In the COMPANY DESCRIPTION portion, provide the reader with an understanding of the current type of business filing(s) (e.g. incorporated, limited liability company, sole proprietorship, etc.). Also, include the mission statement and mandate. Outline the different media in which the business will operate, continuing into a sentence or two that illustrates the planned direction of the organization for the next few years. Close this section with the most current mailing address and contact information of the business and key figure heads.

Create a CORPORATE MANAGEMENT section, introducing the reader to the founders and other noteworthy participants in the business. Then, list the same individuals and their titles. From there, work into a detailed description of the persons listed above, explaining their involvement, experience, qualifications and supplementary information.

In the FACILITIES section, summarize the plan for any necessary office and warehouse space including the types of space (e.g. Class A, Class B, etc.) and rough locations. Next, breakdown all the needs and risks associated with the acquisition. This helps the reader understand that your organization has thought out the idea and understands all facets of the undertaking in a bulleted manner. Following the bulleted list, insert a detailed plan, breaking down the step-by-step tentative plan that you will put in place to procure the space needed.

In the PRIMARY PRODUCT/SERVICE section, introduce the reader to any product(s)/service(s) that are the focal point of the organization's business model. Explain the idea behind the primary product/service and what makes it a value to the potential customers. Also, why is it better than products/services offered by the competition? Follow this introduction with individual breakdowns of each product/service if multiples exist.

In the MARKETING STRATEGIES section, describe the overall marketing plan that the business intends to implement. Include any pertinent demographic research and industry disparities. Touch on the different segments and how you plan to approach them. Include a local, regional, national/international and web-based marketing plan. In these individual paragraphs, discuss the media to be used, including changes that may arise from budget deficits.

Following the individual marketing plan paragraphs, separately discuss the different marketing and advertising efforts that are expected to take place within each facet of media. If a website is in the plan, this is where an outline of its development should be presented, including consumer imagery, functionality and search engine optimization (SEO).

In the FUTURE PLANNING section, take this opportunity to educate your reader on the direction your team plans to take the business. Make this section read like an internal document, similar to an employee handbook. Give a synopsis of future sales expectations, expansion of the marketing plan, and employee growth. This is where well thought-out ideas regarding streamlining production, promotion and distribution are presented (consider outsourcing, private labeling, licensing, trademarking, and franchising).

The final section, FINANCIALS, is the most crucial to the success of your new business. Create this document to ensure that the reader believes that you have done the appropriate research and financial planning to start and operate your business. Include all fixed and variable expenses, then complement these numbers with all expected revenue sources. After producing a written summary of these items, you will need to prepare the necessary expense reports, including balance sheets, income statements, statements of cash flow, and pro forma income statements. Please note that when making the appropriate estimates, offer a breakdown, including both the monetary financials. Also, try to quantify certain pieces; this helps readers that may have been exposed to different schools of thought fully understand your documents.

Any copies of your business plan should be controlled and ensure that you keep a distribution record. This will allow you to update and maintain your business plan on an as-needed basis. Remember, too, that you should include a private placement disclaimer with your business plan if you plan to use it to raise capital.

* * *

Chapter 10

Necessary Components of an Effective Business Plan

(The much longer version)

Having to write a business plan is the most important facet of starting a business. Consequently, it's also the greatest deterrent. Fear not.

* * *

WHEN STARTING A BUSINESS, the very first thing you should have is a business plan. The business plan has several purposes. It's a good way to put ideas on paper and keep track of the steps you've taken to start the business. It's also a major requirement in acquiring financing for your business. No one is going to want to give you any money to help you start your business unless you can prove to them that you have a plan to keep your business from crashing down soon after takeoff. Below, you will find a series of sections that make up a basic business plan.

* * *

The EXECUTIVE SUMMARY is the first part of a business plan and is the most crucial piece of your plan. It provides a very descript synopsis of the entire plan, along with a brief history of your company. This portion of the plan tells readers where your business is and where you want to take it. It's the first thing your readers see; therefore, it is the thing that will both grab their attention and make them want to keep learning or make them want to close the cover and move on to something else. Most importantly, this part of the plan conveys the message of why you believe your business will be successful.

Here's a tip: The Executive Summary is most easily and effectively written at the end of your efforts of planning and writing the business plan. Once all of the details of your plan are in order, you will be prepared to condense it into the Executive Summary. Try to keep this section to fewer than four pages.

Included in the Executive Summary are:

- Mission Statement: The Mission Statement briefly explains the focus of your business. The statement can be any length as long as the point is conveyed and understood. It should be as direct and to-the-point as possible and it should leave the reader with a clear picture of what your business is all about

- When the business was started

- Key management and their roles

- Number of Employees

- Primary location of the business and other satellite locations

- Description of office, manufacturing plant, or facilities

- The products or services

- Current investor information and any additional financial relationships or arrangements

- Brief summary of the company's financial accomplishments and any noteworthy market activities (e.g., your business tripled its value in a one-year period or you became the leader in your industry by developing a certain product)

- Briefly describe management's plans for the business' future. With the exception of the Mission Statement, the information located in the Executive Summary should be represented in a brief or bulleted style. Note that this information is expanded upon in greater detail within the remainder of the business plan

It's not uncommon that if you are just starting a business, you, most likely, will not have a lot of information to populate the fields mentioned above. As an alternative, focus on your experience, background, and the decisions that led you to start the business. Ensure that it contains information about the difficulties your target market has and what resolutions your business will provide. Explain how the business you have will allow you to make meaningful advances into the market. Advise your reader what you're going to perform uniquely or more effectively than your competition. Assure the reader that there is a definite need for the product or service provided by your business, then go ahead and address the business' prospective plans.

To help the reader in pinpointing specific sections within your business plan, provide a table of contents immediately following the Executive Summary. Be confident that the content titles are very broad; try not to include too much detail.

* * *

The MARKET ANALYSIS portion is Part 2 of a well-written business plan. This part of the plan should demonstrate your knowledge regarding the particular industry that your business plans to engage. It should also provide basic statistics and key information of any marketing research data you have obtained; however, the itemized details of your market research studies should be placed in the Appendix section of the business plan.

This part of the business plan should include a description of the industry, target market facts and information, market test results, timeframes, and an evaluation of your competition.

The Industry Description section should include an overview of your primary industry, industry size, current and trailing growth rates, market trends and characteristics relating to the entire industry (for example, what is the lifecycle stage of the industry? What is the industry's expected growth rate?), and include the major customer groups within the industry (businesses, governments, women over 35 years of age, children under 5, etc.). This can be broad or narrow, depending on the size and scope of the industry and the business represented.

The business' target market is the customer base that it wants to supply products or provide services to. When defining a target market, it's vital to narrow the group to a realistic volume. Often, businesses make the fatal miscalculation of trying to offer something to everybody. This approach typically ends in failure.

Within the Target Market section, you should gather information that identifies the following:

- Key characteristics of the primary group you are targeting. This segment should include information about the critical needs of your future customers, the level to which those needs are currently being met, and the demographics of the group. Ensure you also include the geographic location of your target market; identify the key decision-makers, and any seasonal or cyclical trends that may impact the industry or your business model.

- Size of the target market. Herein, you will need to know the amount of available customers in your primary market, the amount of annual purchases they make relative to products or services at par with your own, the geographic area they inhabit, and the expected market growth for this group.

- The magnitude to which your business expects to obtain market-share and the reasons why. When gathering this information, you need to decide how much market share and how many customers you expect to gain in a specific geographic region. In addition, you should provide the reader with an understanding of the reasoning that was used in developing these estimates.

- Pricing and gross margin expectations. In this section, it would be wise to define the structure of your pricing, your gross margin (break-even) requirements, and any discounts or incentives that you plan to offer through the business, such as large-volume purchasing, bulk discounts, or prompt payment discounts that discourage customers from taking advantage of payment terms.

- Target market research and information sources. These resources could be purchased demographic research, directories, business associations, industry publications, and government documents.

- <u>Media</u> the business will use to reach the target audience. The media may include internet marketing, internet radio, terrestrial radio, television, magazines, periodicals, or any other type of engaging media that has potential interaction with the target audience.

- <u>Buying patterns</u> of your target market. The first step is to identify the needs of the potential consumers, conduct research in order to address their needs, review the possibilities, and identify the person or persons that can select the most effective solution.

- <u>Trends</u> that affect the potential customers, coupled with fundamental features of the subsequent markets. As with the primary target market, it is important to pinpoint the needs, demographics and developing trends that are going to affect the secondary markets later.

Including information about any of the market tests already completed is important to include in the business plan. Specific details should be included in the Appendix. Market studies usually include the target customers who were contacted, all data or information that was provided to prospective customers, how critical satisfying their needs really are, and the target market's willingness to purchase products or services at a blend of different price-points from your business.

Lead-time is the required amount of time from when a customer places an order until the moment the product or service is delivered. When you research this information, determine your lead-times regarding initial orders, re-orders, and bulk purchases.

While conducting a competitive analysis (SWOT Analysis) it is critical to identify the competition's product-lines or services and market segment. Use this information to determine their strengths and weaknesses, understand the relationship between your target market and your competitors, and identify any roadblocks that may interfere with you entering the marketplace. Also, be certain that you identify all of the primary competitors for each of the products or services offered. For each key competitor, determine their market share; try to predict when new competitors will enter into the marketplace. In fewer words, how long will your window of opportunity last? Finally, pinpoint any additional or less impactful competitors that may have an effect on your business succeeding.

The strengths or competitive advantages realized by your competition's organization can become advantages that you too provide. These strengths can be found in many different areas of the business. They typically include:

- An ability to service customers' needs

- The holding of a great deal of market share (consumer's brand awareness comes with that)

- Years in business as a trusted organization

- Great financial position, ensuring that they can survive as a business through thick-and-thin

- Exceptional management or personnel

Weaknesses are easy to understand as they are simply the opposite of strengths. However, it is important to analyze the same areas as you did prior in order to determine the weaknesses of your competition. Do they satisfy the needs of their customers? What is their current market penetration? How well do the target audiences and the public view them in regard to past-performance, trust, and reputability? Are they experiencing financial constraints or limitations? These could all be red flags for any business. If you discover weak spots in the competition, try to develop an understanding as to why the problems exist, leaving you with the ability to avoid them.

In the event that target audience is not shared by your competition, you should be able to grow your idea with little resistance. However, if the competition is hungry for your target market, too, you should plan to handle the known roadblocks on your way to success. Some issues you may uncover include:

- Large start-up costs

- Significant time required to get your idea off the ground

- Constantly evolving technologies

- Shortage of skillful personnel

- Customers are unfamiliar with your company, product or

service

- Current intellectual property laws such as patents and trademarks inhibit your ability to innovate

The last section that requires research is the section covering restrictions and regulations. This includes information related to employees, customers, government regulation requirements, and any other future changes. Important items that need to be addressed include: steps necessary to conform to the requirements that are going to affect your business, as well as the timeframe required, such as: When does your business have to be in compliance? On what date do these changes take effect? What will it take, in regard to labor and expenses, to conform to these issues?

* * *

COMPANY DESCRIPTION is Part 3 when compiling a business plan. While keeping the finer details limited, provide the reader with a brief understanding of how all of the different components of the business work in conjunction with one another. A company description typically provides information about the fundamentals of the business, along with a breakdown of the key factors that will lead to the business' success.

When providing the fundamentals of the business, it is important to include detail on the needs of the marketplace that you are trying to satisfy. Ensure you provide detail on the initiatives that you expect will satisfy these needs. Lastly, provide a breakdown of key individuals and major organizations that have these needs.

Fundamental factors of success typically include an ability to satisfy your customers' needs better than the competition, time and cost-effective processes of providing products or services, valuable personnel, and quite often, a prime location. Any, or all, of these provides businesses a competitive advantage.

* * *

ORGANIZATION & MANAGEMENT is Part 4 to a well-written business plan. This section provides profiles of key members of management. At a minimum, it should include the structure of the organization, profiles of key management and Board of Directors (if you have one), and other important ownership information.

The initial subsection of the Organization & Management portion of the business plan should be a structure of the organization. The most effective and cleanest way to show the company's structure is to provide readers with an organizational chart and narrative description. This will demonstrate to your readers that you leave nothing to chance, there is a comprehensive plan in place, and that the most appropriate employee is in charge of each function of the business. Potential investors and employees alike find this to be very important.

Profiles of key management typically follow the organization's structure. What are the individual roles and responsibilities for members of management? What are their education and employment backgrounds and why are they being brought into the business as a member of the board or senior manager? The details may appear unnecessary in one- or two-person businesses; however, individuals, especially investors, reading the business plan, expect to know everyone's role and level of experience. Provide a well thought-out, detailed write-up, including the function of each department or facet of the business.

Again, if you have a Board of Directors, make sure to list all of the members and how you expect to keep them involved with your organization. What salary and benefits packages do you plan to offer employees? Are there any incentive opportunities? Promotions?

One of the most important components for success in the growth of any company is the ability and track record of its owner/management team. Let your readers know about the key people in your company and their backgrounds. Provide resumes that include the following information:

- Name
- Position (include brief position description along with primary duties)
- Primary responsibilities and authority
- Education
- Unique experience and skills
- Prior employment

- Special skills
- Past track record
- Industry recognition
- Community involvement
- Number of years with the company
- Compensation basis and levels (make sure these are reasonable—not too high or too low)

Ensure you quantify achievements (e.g. "Managed a sales force of ten people," "Managed a department of fifteen people," "Increased revenue by 15% in the first six months," "Expanded the retail outlets at the rate of two each year," "Improved the customer service as rated by our customers from a 60% to a 90% rating").

Also, highlight how the people surrounding you complement your own skills. If you're just starting out, show how each person's unique experience will contribute to the success of your venture.

While not all businesses have a Board of Directors, the major benefit of an unpaid advisory board is that it can provide expertise that your company cannot otherwise afford. A list of well-known, successful business owners/managers can go a long way toward enhancing your company's credibility and perception of management expertise.

If you have a Board of Directors, be sure to gather the following information when developing the outline for your business plan:

- Names
- Positions on the board
- Extent of involvement with the company
- Background
- Historical and future contribution to the company's success

Finally, conclude this section by providing details regarding the legal structure of the business, followed by the ownership information. Is the business incorporated? What type of incorporation? Maybe you have an LLC or partnership. Are you are setup as a sole proprietor?

The following ownership information is important and necessary for the Organizational Structure section of a successful business plan:

- Owners' names

- Member interest breakdown (who owns how much)

- Company involvement

- Ownership types (such as common and preferred stock, general partner, limited partner)

- Any other existing equity equivalents such as warrants, options, convertible debt, etc.

- Common stock

* * *

MARKETING AND SALES STRATEGIES is Part 5 of your business plan. Marketing is the process of creating customers: the lifeblood of your business. In this section, the first thing you want to do is define your marketing strategy. There is no single way to approach a marketing strategy. Your strategy should be part of an ongoing business-evaluation process and unique to your company. However, there are common steps you can follow to help you think through the direction and tactics you would like to use to drive sales and sustain customer loyalty.

An overall marketing strategy should include, at a minimum, these four strategies:

- A market penetration strategy

- A growth strategy. This strategy for building your business might include an internal strategy such as how to increase your human resources, an acquisition strategy such as buying another business, a franchise strategy for branching out, a horizontal strategy where you would provide the same type of products to different users, or a vertical strategy where you would continue providing the same products but would offer them at different levels of the distribution chain

- Channels of distribution strategy. Choices for distribution channels could include original equipment manufacturers (OEM's), an internal sales force, distributors, or retailers

- Communication strategy. How are you going to reach your customers? Usually, a combination of the following tactics works the best: promotions, advertising, public relations, personal selling, and printed materials such as brochures, catalogs, flyers, etc.

After you have developed a comprehensive marketing strategy, you can then define your sales strategy. This covers how you plan to actually sell your product(s).

Your overall sales strategy should include two primary elements:

- A sales force strategy. If you are going to have a sales force, do you plan to use internal or independent representatives? How many salespeople will you recruit for your sales force? What type of recruitment strategies will you use? How will you train your sales force? What about compensation for your sales force?

- Your sales activities. When you are defining your sales strategy, it is important that you break it down into activities. For instance, you need to identify your prospects. Once you have made a list of your prospects, you need to prioritize the contacts, selecting the leads with the highest potential to buy first. Next, identify the number of sales calls you will make over a certain period of time. From there, you need to determine the average number of sales calls you will need to make per sale, the average dollar size per sale, and the average dollar size per vendor

* * *

SERVICE OR PRODUCT LINE is Part 6 of your business plan. What are you selling? In this section, describe your service or product, emphasizing the benefits to potential and current customers. For example, don't tell your readers which 89 foods you carry in your "Gourmet to Go" shop. Tell them why busy, two-career couples will prefer shopping in a service-oriented store that records clients' food preferences and caters to even the smallest parties on short notice.

Focus on the areas where you have a distinct advantage. Identify the problem in your target market for which your service or product provides a solution. Give the reader hard evidence that people are, or will be, willing to pay for your solution. List your company's services and products and attach any marketing/promotional materials. Provide details regarding suppliers, availability of products/services, and service or product costs. Also include information addressing new services or products which will soon be added to the company's line.

Overall, this section should include:

- A detailed description of your product or service (from your customers' perspective). You should include information about the specific benefits of your product or service. You should also talk about your product/service's ability to meet consumer needs, any advantages your product has over that of the competition, and the present development stage your product is in (e.g. idea, prototype, etc.).

- Information related to your product's life cycle. Ensure to include information about where your product or service is in its life cycle, as well as any factors that may influence its cycle in the future.

- Any copyright, patent and trade secret information that may be relevant. This should include information related to existing, pending or anticipated copyright and patent filings along with any key characteristics of your products/services for which you cannot obtain a copyright or patent. This is where you should also incorporate key aspects of your products/services that may be classified as trade secrets. Last, but not least, be sure to add any information pertaining to existing legal agreements, such as nondisclosure or non-compete agreements.

- Research and development (R&D) activities you are

involved in or are planning to be involved in. These would include any in-process or future activities related to the development of new products/services. This section would also include information about what you expect the results of future R&D activities to be. Be sure to analyze the R&D efforts of not only your own business, but also that of others in your industry.

* * *

The FUNDING REQUEST is Part 7 of your business plan. In this section, you will request the amount of funding you will need to start or expand your business. If necessary, you can include different funding scenarios, such as best- and worst-case scenarios. Remember that later, in the financial section, you must be able to back up these requests and scenarios with corresponding financial statements.

You will want to include the following in your funding request:

- Your <u>current</u> funding requirement

- Your <u>future</u> funding requirements over the next five years

- <u>How you will use</u> the funds you receive

- Any <u>long-range financial strategies</u> that you are planning that would have any type of impact on your funding request

When you are outlining your current and future funding requirements, ensure you include the amount you want now and the amount you want in the future, the time period that each request will cover, the type of funding you would like to have (e.g. equity, debt), and the terms that you would like to have applied.

How you will use your funds is very important to a creditor. Is the funding requested for capital expenditures? Working capital? Debt retirement? Acquisitions? Whatever it is, be sure to list it in this section.

Last of all, ensure that you include any strategic information related to your business that may have an impact on your financial situation in the future, such as going public with your company, having a leveraged buyout, being acquired by another company, the method with which you will service your debt, or whether or not you plan to sell your business in the future. Each of these is extremely important to a future creditor, since they will directly impact your ability to repay your loan(s).

* * *

FINANCIALS is Part 8 of your business plan. The financials should be developed after you've analyzed the market and set clear, realistic objectives. Only then, can you allocate resources efficiently. The following is a list of the critical financial statements to include in your business plan packet:

Historical Financial Data. If you own an established business, you will be requested to supply historical data related to your company's performance. Most creditors request data for the last three-to-five years, depending on the length of time you have been in business.

The historical financial data you would want to include would be your company's income statements, balance sheets, and cash flow statements for each year you have been in business (usually for up to three-to-five years). Often, creditors are also interested in any collateral that you may have that could be used to ensure your loan, regardless of the stage of your business.

Prospective Financial Data. All businesses, whether start-up or growing, will be required to supply prospective financial data. Most of the time, creditors will want to see what you expect your company to be able to do over the next five years. Each year's documents should include forecasted income statements, balance sheets, cash flow statements, and capital expenditure budgets. For the first year, you should supply monthly or quarterly projections. From there, you can stretch it to quarterly and/or yearly projections for years two-through-five.

Ensure that your projections match your funding requests. Creditors will be on the lookout for inconsistencies. It's much better if you catch mistakes before they do. If you have made assumptions in your projections, be sure to summarize what you have assumed. This way, the reader will not be left guessing.

Finally, include a short analysis of your financial information. Include a ratio and trend analysis for all of your financial statements (both historical and prospective). Since pictures speak louder than words, you may want to add graphs of your trend analysis (especially if they are positive).

* * *

The APPENDIX, Part 9, is the final section of your business plan that you should prepare. However, this section should be provided to readers on an as-needed basis. In other words, it should *not* be included with the main body of your business plan. Your plan is your communication tool; as such, it will be seen by a lot of people. Some of the information in the business section you will not want everyone to see. Specific individuals (such as creditors) may want access to this information in order to make lending decisions. Therefore, it is important to have the Appendix within easy reach.

The Appendix should include:

- Credit history (personal & business)
- Resumes of key managers
- Product pictures
- Letters of reference
- Details of market studies
- Relevant magazine articles or book references
- Licenses, permits or patents
- Legal documents
- Copies of leases
- Building permits
- Contracts
- List of business consultants, including attorney and accountant

Any copies of your business plan should be controlled and ensure that you keep a distribution record. This will allow you to update and maintain your business plan on an as-needed basis. Remember, too, that you should include a private placement disclaimer with your business plan if you plan to use it to raise capital.

* * *

Chapter 11

A.T.N.A. (All Talk No Action)

No one ever accomplished their goal by doing a whole lot of nothing.

* * *

HAVE YOU EVER, while sitting in a room with friends or colleagues who are discussing a new business idea or job opportunity, said to yourself, "I've heard this record before!"? Sure—we all have. It's a perfect example of the biggest bottleneck when it comes to achievement, productivity and success. Every time I hear someone say that they're "going to do" something, and I've heard it several times before, it's all I can do to not stand up on my chair and holler at them, "So, do it already!"

It's sad, but so many individuals genuinely have great business ideas that, if implemented, could truly change their lives. However, it's unfortunate that most of those people are too busy getting ready to get ready. They can usually be found sitting around a coffee shop or a local watering hole handing out their latest initiative's business cards and marketing materials while talking all-the-while about how successful they will soon be and that it's only going to take a few months of planning and execution before they get "there."

These people crack me up. It seems like every 3-6 months, they are spending $500-1,500 on screen-printed T-shirts, pens, magnets, etc., when if they would simply stick with one thing for more than ten minutes, they would have something—something truly significant! The bottom line is the majority of businesses don't fail because of the product, service or idea, but because of the lack of dedication, follow-through and willingness to put rubber to the road.

Don't get caught in the loop. Make it happen!

Instead of "the loop," focus on the realities at hand. Although it is important to think through all of the risks or potential issues associated with a venture, it is equally important to revisit the idea or widget that got you excited in the first place and take yourself to the proverbial 30,000-foot aerial view to recognize that, quite often, you are over thinking the details. Don't be afraid to go back to basics, especially if it helps qualify the viability of the whole idea.

I'll be the first to admit that I've been there. I'm the guy that used to reduce everything down to the most insignificant detail trying to find the flaws when in reality, what I was focusing on was so far away from the main idea that days, weeks and months would fly by and by the time I would come up for air, I was so burned-out running through the idea from all directions, that I didn't even have an interest anymore, nor did I think the idea would work. Remember, I'm not trying to say the details aren't important, I'm simply saying that sometimes you need to focus on the whole plate, not each individual pea, and don't be afraid of the first step toward your goal.

* * *

Chapter 12

Prioritizing Your Way to Success

Don't get out too far over your skis unless you want to slide down the mountain on your face. Here are some helpful tips.

* * *

EVERYBODY PLANS—It's a part of our lives and human nature. When you go to the grocery store, you make a list. When you go shopping, you have things that you want in mind. The question now is: How long does it take you to accomplish those tasks? Do you spend an hour in the grocery store because you go down the list from top to bottom, ignoring the order of your groceries' placement in the store? Or do you shop smart, bring a pencil, and go from one side of the store to the other, checking your items off the list as you go?

Shopping habits aside, let's convert this scenario for usage in a corporate setting. With today's economy, changes are, if you have a job, you're probably overworked and feel like your tasks are never fully accomplished. If you're an entrepreneur trying to start your own business, you know you have to accomplish a seemingly endless number of tasks in order to get your operation off the ground or grown to the next level. Have you finished writing your business plan? Have you researched funding options? Have you planned how you're going to go public? Do you have enough employee help or farmed out resources to get you off the ground and up to a competitive momentum?

If you answered 'yes' to all of those questions, I'm afraid that you're not using your time as wisely as you could. If you're just trying to start a small business and are wasting time thinking about going public, it means that you're not focusing enough on what you should be: the now. It takes years for the average privately owned company to go public or release their initial public offering (IPO). The reason may not be why you think. Think about it from an investor's standpoint; would you give a huge amount of money to a company that had only had its doors open for five minutes? I know I wouldn't—out of principle. Simply stated, successful investors didn't get that way because they were risky or stupid.

Getting back to the point, if you're focusing on tasks that don't need pondering for another five years, then you're not getting done now what needs to happen to get you to that five-year point. We call it, "getting out over your skis." If you're whipping down a steep bank and lean too far forward, you're going to end up flat on your face.

The solution is to stick to the now and prioritize. If you need to make a gigantic list (as I often do), then do so. After I've made my list, I often sub-categorize my list in order to break my list into major (often profit-bearing) accomplishments, and the tasks that each requires. That way, I can focus on one project and ensure that I accomplish everything I need to in order to prove that initiative profitable.

If this concept is still a little unclear and you're a fan of 1950's dramatic theater, the "or" title to this chapter would be, "The Case of the Entrepreneur Who Spread Himself Too Thin and Accomplished Nothing."

* * *

Chapter 13

The Importance of Market Testing

Would you dive into a body of water if you couldn't see below the surface? The same concept applies here.

* * *

MY WIFE HAS a burning desire to open a bakery in our community. She watched one of those reality shows about an independently owned bakery and how much fun it was for some sisters (she has two) to own a bakery together, and how popular the bakery was, and how much money they made, and all the beautiful people that were constantly flowing in and out of the bakery all day long. In the episode that I watched five minutes of, it really looked like heaven on earth for those reality TV sisters and their glorious bakery.

In support of my wife, I will admit that she creates the most delicious cakes and treats that I have ever tasted, and I'm a pretty well-travelled (and well-fed) guy. I need to preface the rest of this article by stating that all else being equal, my wife's culinary skills are unquestionably a very marketable product. It wasn't her skills, however, that was blocking my full support of this endeavor.

We live in a relatively small town, about thirty minutes away from the nearest big city. There aren't a lot of foot-trafficable areas and aside from a few, small, wealthy congregations, the average state of wealth isn't very high. While our community is by no means impoverished, it's not fancy either. After she mentioned that she wanted to open a small bakery, I spent some time on Google and looked up every small bakery in our area. After spending a couple hours driving by every one and checking out their operations, I wasn't convinced that an independent bakery was the wisest endeavor. While the bakeries weren't shabby, they didn't look profitable either. You can typically tell when a small business is doing well and when one isn't by spending time in their establishment, after all.

Not quite ready to give up on my wife's dream, I went home to consult with my old friend, Google again. This time, I looked up the tax information (public record) of each of the bakeries, as well as the average cost of rent and purchase for retail space with existing kitchen equipment functional and installed in our area. While the claimed income (from the tax info) for the bakeries was more than I expected it would be, it was the cost of the real estate that blew me away.

While a privately owned bakery *could* be profitable, the general populace in our community couldn't afford what my wife and her sisters would have to charge for their treats to be able to keep the bakery's doors open for business. $8 cupcakes might fly in the "big city," but they don't in my humble community where the majority of its citizens are on retiree fixed budgets.

The bottom line, in this case, is that desserts are a luxury. They could be the most delicious desserts in the world, but if people can't afford to pay what they will cost, there isn't much else anyone can do.

Ideas for making this work, however, include catering and/or delivery to neighboring communities (to broaden your customer base) or perhaps even international dry-ice shipping (to broaden your customer base even more).

The moral of the story is that even great business ideas and stellar products don't work everywhere. Too often, people spend too much time focusing on their supply, and not enough on the demand. In short, if no one's there to buy, you won't be selling anything. I'm not trying to crush anyone's dreams here; all I'm saying is that you would be wise to do your due diligence before you launch an endeavor and research what *your* market will bear.

* * *

Chapter 14

No Job, No Opps, Now What?

It's not 2004, not everyone can make 100K a year anymore! Don't hang out to dry!

* * *

IN A DOWN ECONOMY, with the job market already flooded with qualified, educated and motivated interviewees, don't think for a second that you can stand around, slide by, or step into a business' hierarchy without getting down into a three-point stance and tackling what needs your attention in regard to relationship-building, continued education, and resume preparation.

You don't want to compete in an over-saturated job market, nor do you want to take a position with a company that lacks feelings of fulfillment—I get it. Just remember that every problem is an opportunity in disguise. This may be the perfect time for you to circle back around to that business idea you've always had or the business you've always wanted to start with your friends.

Ask yourself, what are the next 5-10 critical steps? Make sure to write them down and include as much off-the-cuff detail as you can about each one. Next, estimate how much time is required to complete each task on that list. Write these ballpark figures next to each item. At this point, you're ready to start building your business' base. Compare the amount of time required to complete each task with the hours of free time available in your typical week. Now set some realistic deadlines for yourself. This may sound stupid but I will assure you that deadlines tend to cure most cases of procrastination. To give it to you straight, the person that says, "I'll figure it out," will be saying the same thing at the same time next year.

Once you've completed the first round of tasks, it will probably be necessary to repeat the process. Don't get frustrated. This won't go on forever, but you will most likely discover a fresh list of tasks necessary for completion. You're not short-sighted; this is normal. At this point, you should be ready to get your feet wet. Once this point is reached, a lot of people, surprisingly, shelf their initiative. Why? I don't know, probably because they are burned out from all the boring, tedious and time-consuming steps that got them this far.

Get excited! You've just taken your idea from a mere concept to what is now a fully conceptualized, well thought-out, flushed-out, qualified, strategized and structured business model. In my opinion, this is the fun part. Go out and market yourself and your product or service. Take my advice that once you've gained good momentum to go out and start that business you've always wanted, you'll find it much easier to continue. The most important thing is not to quit when it gets tough, and to hold yourself accountable to those self-set deadlines.

* * *

Part II

Getting Financed

Chapter 15

How to Obtain Business Financing

Unless your new business is a money-tree farm, you will find this chapter very useful.

* * *

WHEN DETERMINING what type of financing to procure for your business, there are many avenues to consider. Depending on the type of business, future plans, and product(s) and service(s) offered, the choice is important. There are two main types of financing debt or equity. Debt financing is the process by which a firm borrows capital from banks and investors, promising to repay the borrowed funds within a certain amount of time or incur some type of liability, usually in the form of interest. The other type is equity financing, when an organization relinquishes ownership interest to different sources in exchange for capital. Most well-capitalized businesses use a balance of both; this helps mitigate risk and keep the cost of capital to a minimum.

Debt financing is usually done by businesses that have either established positive cash flow or have the necessary collateral (equipment, cash or an individual's promissory note) to secure the funds from a lender. When businesses choose this method, it is obligated to pay a carrying cost on the funds. This is common among businesses that either deal in large volume inventory purchases that are later liquidated through sales channels, thus keeping the term of the loan to a minimum, or businesses that need to expand by purchasing space or equipment with a liquidation value similar to the debt outstanding (real estate, long-term-use equipment, and vehicles).

Having such a risk-free connotation, equity financing can be a great tool when expanding beyond the size and scope of what could be accomplished with conventional debt financing. In exchange for interest in the organization, a firm can raise excess capital while only being exposed with a few key liabilities. First, a firm must worry about who holds the controlling interest (takeovers, buyouts). Also, depending on the way in which the interest was conveyed, individuals can recoup their investment through multiple channels. This is when contracts detailing cash capital disbursements are important. Lastly, remember that there is a strong correlation between risk and reward. For this section, that statement is referring to the reality that if a firm relinquishes a good portion of its interest to other investors, the original owners may only be entitled to a portion of the profits, in the event that the organization performs extremely well.

There are many different types of private investors and investment groups. The most common is the accredited investor. These individuals are familiar with the investment world and have probably participated in such ventures previously. They also have certain qualifications to make them an attractive financier. Also, another type is an angel investor. This term has a loose meaning but basically labels an individual who has the excess expendable income to almost entirely fund the start-up, expansion or growth of a business. Both accredited investors and angel investors are private participates that are not usually affiliated with an investment group.

Then, there are investment groups, such as venture capitalists (VC's). Venture capital groups are great for companies that are interested in retaining brain-trust equity and/or a portion of the control, but not all. These groups tend to know exactly what they are looking for from their involvement. The forfeiture of controlling interest and substantial portions of revenue is not uncommon. However, by using such groups, a business' current owners can nearly eliminate their financial risk. Due to the venture capitalists having a vested interest, expect the participation of seasoned business consultants that will take a 'hands-on approach' and work with the firm to achieve success.

Some businesses have the ability to approach the public through an initial public offering (IPO). This is the process by which a company works with investment bankers to build a following in a specific trading platform, then offer interest in the company on its behalf, in exchange for a portion of the proceeds. There can be great benefits as well as detriments associated with making an initial public offering. The most commonly understood perk is that, on average, a firm can collect ten times its value in one offering and in special circumstances, either the product or service is groundbreaking or there is a large emotional following in the market. In these cases, an organization can raise exponentially more. This was seen during the dot-com era, in the late nineties, when technology companies were making initial public offerings and the stock prices were driven up thousands of percent above book value, simply because of speculation of success.

The small business administration (SBA) can be an excellent source of capital. Especially for new businesses, they offer competitive loans, grants and subsidies. However, the majority of the funds are only released to businesses or individuals with specific qualifications, such as minorities, persons with disabilities, and individuals coming from a low socioeconomic background. When working this avenue for funding, you will encounter numerous waiting periods that can only be expedited by spending more money. Most of the forms necessary for different filings can be filled out digitally and submitted online, or they can be downloaded, printed and then faxed to the necessary recipient.

Before searching for financing, a good idea is to see what federal grants are available or you might qualify for. Grants will keep you from losing ownership or incurring debt. There are many different ways to acquire financing. Preparation and research will pay off well for you.

* * *

Chapter 16

Financing Your Business

(Further guidance)

When seeking financial backing from an outside source, ask yourself: Which is best for my company?

* * *

THERE ARE MANY DIFFERENT METHODS of obtaining financing for your business. You can select to acquire financing from a venture capitalist group, angel investors, the bank, or even a close family member or friends. You have to find out the eligibility requirements of each of the four groups so you can determine which form of financing is best suited for your company.

The primary similarity between venture capitalist groups, angel investors, and bank financing is that the three parties can go a long way in helping a business get started and increase momentum without the risk of putting personal relationships in jeopardy. Below are the other similarities and differences.

Venture capitalist groups are organizations that will normally invest capital in an already operating business as they prefer to alleviate risk by investing in companies that are already financially stable. They typically offer short-term investments for up to five years. Unlike other investors, venture capitalists only expect returns on their investments and have little or no interest in co-owning the business. When considering the three options of financing and which is best for you and your company, you should rule-out venture capitalists if you are just starting out or are still in the conceptual stages. This is simply because, more often than not, they won't invest in new un-established businesses. They will expect you to have a business plan put together; also, be prepared to hand over financials as well, including a report on how you managed your finances over the past 3-5 years. They will also have someone employed in their company to analyze and evaluate everything that your company has done and will do in the foreseen future, just to make sure that they have a firm grasp on, and understanding of, their investment and are aware of all that is taking place on a day-to-day basis.

If you are just starting a new business and trying to acquire financing, you have an elevated chance of getting the amount you desire from an **angel investor**. An angel investor (also known as a "business angel" or "informal investor") is an individual who provides capital for a business start-up, usually in exchange for convertible debt or ownership equity. A small, but increasing, number of angel investors organize themselves into angel groups or angel networks to share research and pool their investing. These investors normally invest in new businesses that look promising. They can be individuals or organizations. They may ask for their returns or alternatively ask to be co-owners of the business. Angel investors make long-term investments unlike the venture capitalist groups. The investment amount may range from hundreds to thousands, or even millions of dollars, depending on the kind of investor(s) that you manage to approach.

You can also acquire **bank financing** for your business. If you have an established business that has been in operation for a period of time, this is another good option. The bank will consider your financial statements and credit history in order to get you a loan. Sometimes, they may elect to give you a smaller loan than you had first requested, depending on your financial status and the bank policies. When you are applying for a bank loan, some of the things that you should take into consideration include interest rates and re-payment periods. Always remember to read the fine print. Different banks have different interest rates, so make sure you do your due-diligence and research the best rates and can pay back the amount in a short period of time.

Be cognizant that banks may not offer loans to businesses that are just starting out. This is because they consider these loans to be high-risk, with the probability of having difficulties when it comes time to pay the loan back. However, if you provide collateral for the loan, the bank may re-consider. Some of the collateral that you can provide can include business assets, title deeds, car logbooks, and any other assets that they may be able to use as collateral against your loan. Keep in mind, that if you fail to repay the loan, you will lose whatever you provided as collateral.

If you feel that you are able to work with your **friends and family**, and you have friends and family members with the resources to finance your business, you should consider them as a method of financing your business. Working with family can be rewarding and challenging at the same time; it's sometimes hard to mix business with your personal life, but if you can persuade your family to advance you a loan at a better rate than the banks, then you are saving the accumulated interest that you would have acquired by using an alternative form of loan (you never know, they might not charge you any interest at all). If they do choose to charge you interest, use financing agreements as you would with any other investor, and outline the payment terms and interest rate your family has agreed to.

Also, make sure you both understand all terms of the contract so there won't be a discrepancy and cause tension within the family or friendship. If you run into financial problems with your company, your chances are much higher to being able to re-negotiate the terms of your loan to save your business with family members than with a bank or VC group.

When deciding between a venture capitalist group, angel investors, or bank financing, and considering which option is the best for you and your company, it is highly recommended that you research all of your options. Go through all of the eligibility and terms requirements and weigh-out the pros-and-cons for all of your potential investors and see what the best option for your business is.

* * *

Chapter 17

The Transformation of Lending in America

As the access door to lending closes, American small businesses are seeking capital elsewhere. Here's why.

* * *

ONE OF THE SINGLE greatest frustrations for small businesses in America is limited access to capital. A few years ago, entrepreneurs could approach traditional banks with business plans, projections, and a good credit history, and secure reasonable financing under favorable terms in short order. Today, the requirements for underwriting the same loan are so difficult that conventional bank lending is limited to a much smaller percentage that qualifies. This reality is causing a necessary shift in the lending environment.

Traditional banks will begin to see loan requests diminish more and more as entrepreneurs and small businesses pursue alternate sources for capital. One emerging source is private placement capital from individuals who prefer to loan capital to small businesses at higher interest rates than they have been receiving from bank deposit accounts or investment accounts. With the proper presentation and disclosure of the small business performance and opportunity, a private individual often finds the premium interest rate provided by the small business a welcome change from current traditional alternatives. In some cases, these lending programs can grow into opportunities for permanent investment into the small business. The interesting point about this new lending option is that banks may diminish their lending portfolio while simultaneously reducing their customer deposit accounts with those who choose to fund these loans.

The larger scale opportunity for funding is with venture capital resources that often search for emerging businesses that present an opportunity for a substantial return in a specific timeframe. These sources often prefer a business that has been around long enough to establish some element of momentum or proof of concept. Each source may have different business sectors in which they specialize because of their core expertise. If your business is within their core focus and meets the guidelines they target for scale and future potential, there may be a good fit. The fundamental point to remember is that they are often interested in a 20% annual return on their investment. This means that either through interest, dividend or equity sale, they like to fund a program where they can see substantial financial results in 3-7 years. The key to using these sources is related to the strength of the financial opportunity if these funds are provided. Rapid growth models with large payoffs upon execution are typical for these sources of capital.

There are sources that fall between the large venture capital source and the small individual private source. Certain individuals and businesses that specialize in target investing at a scale less than typical venture capital sources are often referred to as "Angel Investors." These sources often consider mid-range amounts and have more flexibility in how they approach an investment. There may be broader options for length of term, method of return, elements of equity, and other variables to a deal.

The common element that seems to be present in more popular lending sources for small businesses and entrepreneurs is a greater focus and weight on the prospective elements of the opportunity than the retrospective results of the business. In traditional bank lending, the greater focus is clearly on the retrospective financial performance as the primary qualifier that is supported by business and personal creditworthiness. Prospective elements of the opportunity are simply an accent to the process and of very little importance in the loan underwriting by traditional bank lending.

With traditional bank lending fixated on historical business results, it is not surprising that the forward-looking entrepreneurial spirit that built American small business structure is turning away from traditional banks. As these newer lending resources become the basis for small business funding, traditional banking will continue to erode, causing a transformation of lending in America.

* * *

Chapter 18

So, What's the Deal with Small Business Credit?

Knock, knock. Who's there? Your business' credit score—and it's not a joke.

* * *

CREDIT IS THE MARK that lenders will use to gauge whether your small business qualifies for a loan, as well as the amount (sorry, you might not get the amount you want simply because you've been approved). A system known as FICO (the most common system made by Fair Isaac Corporation) is used to determine credit score in order to evaluate whether a business is eligible for a loan. The system allocates a number, ranging from 300 (ranked extremely poor) to 900 (ranked perfect credit). The majority of businesses fall between 550 and 750 (points). It is worth noting that your FICO score will depend on five aspects: amount owed, payment history, span of credit history, credit history, and the various sorts of credit.

It becomes hard for one to ask for a loan while facing debts. This may be damaging to your credit score. For one to make an improvement to one's credit score, there must be an improvement on the debt-to-income relation; as such, paying off borrowed money can be of help in ensuring a good credit score. One can even consult financial services to improve on the above mentioned ratio and restore the life of the business. For any business, especially small businesses, to realize success, good credit control practice should be a priority. In fact, a good number of small businesses end up being declared bankrupt just because of scanty credit control measures and a questionable position of the administration.

A key reason why credit control is so imperative, as far as a small or a new venture is concerned, is that these businesses find it hard to unlock lines of credit accounts to the suppliers. Most suppliers expect that the lesser business will make straight payments for the supplies purchased, which is not always the case since these hatchling businesses will often lack any other option other than offering an account net of 30 days to customers. For a rapidly growing small business, one will notice that costs of supplies tend to have a proportionate increase.

A good credit score forms the basis of small or new businesses. It puts one in a position to acquire funding for issues such as capital expenditures, expansion, employment creation, research, and extension. It remains a key factor toward the growth of any business and guarantees a promising future.

Nevertheless, good credit allows a business owner to closely monitor cash, thus ensuring that the cost of running a business doesn't become a problem. This kind of liquidity allows one to respond promptly to time-sensitive necessities and that there is no need to halt or compromise processes. Specialized financial advisers can offer advice which helps with establishing, monitoring, improving and protecting your credit.

Aside from helping business owners get access to financial aids, good credit has more often become the chief means to set conditions on business loans, determination of insurance premiums, even allocating lease payments. Finally, good credit can also fetch you reduced rates, reinforcing your flow of cash.

* * *

Part III

Getting Started

Chapter 19

Cycle of Business Balanced with Speed of Business

Finding the perfect cross between planning and execution just got easier.

* * *

ONE OF THE MORE difficult challenges facing businesses today is determining the best balance between preparation and execution of a project or program. Too often, we drag out the preparation of an important initiative, beyond the critical window of time, when it is still effective for the original objective. Alternatively, we may proceed too quickly with an execution and neglect vital preparation details, thus causing us to fail to achieve the objective. What is the correct balance between preparation and execution?

The secret lies in the understanding of the cycle of your business' development or "life-cycle" of your business. Businesses that are just getting started and need to move from square-one to some level of revenue momentum, in order to achieve a financially sustainable position, need to over-execute, even at the risk of more limited preparation. Preparation, however, should never be ignored or slighted in the process. Execution is the critical variable that leads the formula.

When building a start-up business, you organize a plan-of-action and proceed down a path that may require continuous adjustment, until you achieve the necessary outcomes and momentum. This can be frustrating if you need to adjust more times than anticipated, and you expend more capital than planned. I often reflect on a comment from Thomas Edison, who said, "I have learned over a hundred ways how not to make a light bulb." His quote serves as an example of the extensive executions in pure volume that may be required in the initial start-up cycle of a business. Knowing that, in most cases, capital is limited, it is critical to execute a pace that reaches a positive outcome before capital is depleted. Therefore, it is understood that you may need to limit the time in preparation, out of the necessity, to execute more initiatives in the time available with limited capital. In start up, you acquire significant knowledge by taking action. In short, losing small battles and learning from it often wins the war. The key is to learn and adjust, not make the same mistakes repeatedly. Small degrees of preparation shortfalls are more than offset by the ability to execute more initiatives.

As a business matures and becomes more established, the cycle of business needs a different balance to the process. With age comes a new variable: experience. As such, there is more accumulated knowledge from the prior growth of the business. There are likely more established components of the business that would be negatively impacted by any preparation errors with a new initiative. There are more definitive established customers and programs that might be jeopardized by an initiative that is poorly conceived. Therefore, in more established and mature businesses, it is important to be thorough in the preparation process and understand all the complex impacts to the entire existing business model.

The larger danger here is to get so deep into the preparation process that the execution never happens. In these situations, it is imperative to build a project timeline that delineates each step of the preparation process into a definitive deliverable with a specific deadline. Then, at each scheduled deadline, there is an opportunity to assess the continuing viability of the initiative and determine if you will amend the plan, abandon the plan, or continue toward the next step and possible execution. Compartmentalization allows for close examination of each facet, in order to more easily identify issues at a magnified level. The task of trying to identify an issue is much more daunting if a company with multiple divisions or appendages is being analyzed holistically. In more established businesses, this process often moves more slowly because the urgency felt in a start-up business has been replaced with a greater tolerance for planning, meeting, discussing and debating. The key here is to accept the nature of a more elaborate preparation process, but manage it to execution with a clear timeline management process.

The point to remember, regardless of the cycle of your business, is that the speed of business is always relative to where you are in that cycle. If you are struggling to achieve momentum as a start-up, you need to push the envelope on rapid execution, accepting some measured and limited risk in the preparation process. It is all about moving, taking action, and adjusting along the way until you reach a financially sustainable level. In a more established business cycle, you need to protect the core model while you execute new initiatives. A slower pace on execution is acceptable to protect the impact to the core business, but do not let yourself get caught in a failure to execute. A project timeline is a valuable tool to keep the process on track and focused to a conclusion.

* * *

Chapter 20

How to Blue Chip Your Business

When you're just starting out with a new business, you probably lay awake at night wondering if you're making the most of your resources and opportunities. Rest easy with these brilliant options for catapulting your new business to the next level—overnight.

* * *

IN THE BEGINNING, every small business struggles to look like a solid, reputable company. The appearance of stable success helps generate more business by adding a level of credibility and trust in the eyes of your customers. Most of all, it helps small businesses interact with larger players within their industry. Working on a limited budget? Don't lose hope; there are a few easy steps that can be implemented to immediately make a business look solid, successful and professional for little-to-no cost.

A good first step is to go to a UPS Store located in an area of town or a specific city that you would like to have a business address; when you get there, setup a mailbox in your business' name. If it happens to be out of the way for you to get there, simply set up mail forwarding to your actual address. It is important to seek out a UPS Store because they accept mail and packages from all carriers, unlike the post office. Also, remember that if you get a P.O. box from a post office, you will have a PO Box address, which isn't professional-looking at all. If anything, it looks shady and makes people doubt the legitimacy of your business, which is the exact opposite of what you want. How would you like to do business with an organization that advertizes its storefront as a tiny metal box? Most mailboxes set up through UPS stores allow the box owners to use the physical address of the store, followed by the mailbox number written as Suite (#), just the same as if it were a suite in an office building. Most people assume that an office suite is a class "A" office space in a nice part of town. See, you're moving up already!

Another smart move is to setup a VOIP or "Voice-Over Internet Protocol" number. These 1-800 numbers are great because they are very inexpensive and add another professional component to a small business. Most people associate toll-free numbers with larger firms and Fortune 500 companies. Now, with a VOIP number, individuals and small businesses can have toll-free numbers for as low as $9.99 a month through companies like Ring Central.

Virtual Receptionists are the next step to maximizing your phone presence. Most voice-over (VO) specialists charge about $50 for every 75 words. You can hire someone male or female, from anywhere in the world, depending on what type of voice you would like answering for your business. With a foreign-accented message, you've just added an international component to your business. These pre-recorded answering messages can be coupled with interactive response systems that allow callers to enter an extension or select departments from a menu such as "sales, press 1, customer support, press 2," etc.

If you have a website, fantastic! You'll be able to take advantage of this one. Set up contact emails for individual departments or services within your small business. Don't worry about the size of your small business or how many email accounts you setup. This helps give the appearance of a large, compartmentalized company. Best of all, you can forward all of the email addresses into one central account that you can easily check by yourself. For example, sales@yourwebsite.com, support@your website.com, HR@yourwebsite.com, admin@yourwebsite.com, etc. The list can go on and on. Just be realistic and think about what makes the most sense for you and your business.

In about five minutes, you've learned how to place your business anywhere you want, add international notoriety, and add big-business function, all for an extremely low cost to your now-growing small business. You've learned how to take advantage of options that you didn't even know where available to you. Work smarter, not harder!

* * *

Chapter 21

The Failure of Conventional Lending in America

(Sad, but true)

"A bank is a place that will lend you money if you can prove that you don't need it." -Bob Hope

* * *

LOOKING BACK just a few years ago, conventional banks provided the primary capital resources to American entrepreneurs to fuel the growth of small businesses and perpetuate the American dream. Today, that lending environment has changed and the small business arena is struggling to find a new primary capital resource.

As we ended 2008, major financial problems with various financial institutions turned the conventional lending world upside-down. The backlash of regulatory changes and federal government scrutiny of banks and other financial institutions has changed the focus of conventional lending to become almost ridiculous. A typical small business loan under prior guidelines would be evaluated on a balance of retrospective performance, current financials, and prospective business planning to determine qualification for loan approval. Today, a typical small business must demonstrate retrospective performance that virtually guarantees an ability to service the loan while simultaneously showing current financial equity more-than-sufficient to cover the debt. The presence of a strong prospective plan is irrelevant if the prior elements of a virtual guarantee are not in place. What is even more challenging is the fact that one of the two elements is worthless without the second.

Equity in excess of the loan amount is insufficient to secure the loan without the evidence of cash flow that will service the loan. Alternatively, evidence of substantial cash flow that would easily service the loan will fall short of the goal without equity that could offset the loan amount. Even when the two requirements are met, personal guarantees are usually necessary to satisfy the bank loan underwriters. This creates a real dilemma for emerging small business entrepreneurs in America.

The true spirit of the American entrepreneur has always been the element that has set us apart in the world. The capital resources will be found through alternate methods that bypass conventional banking and fuel the emergence of a new method for funding the growth of small business in America. Conventional banking will see the requests for lending shrink and the level and duration of deposit relationships dwindle. Banking in America will become a processing service and lending will become a smaller part of their model.

A new method of distributing capital resources from private sources as loans and/or equity investments directly to small businesses will begin to replace some of the conventional lending. Other new methods of funding small businesses may come from large corporations who provide capital resources to smaller synergistic operations that feed a business need or niche for the larger corporation.

Municipalities may raise funds to provide capital resources to captivate businesses to establish and/or grow in that community. New web-based resources will emerge that connect financial, labor, material, land and facility resources in new dynamic ways that eliminate many of the barriers present in the conventional "brick and mortar" banking environment of today.

The key is to look beyond the constraints of today's conventional lending environment and focus on the diverse sources looking for opportunities to earn more return on their capital than would otherwise be offered to them by conventional banks and other traditional financial investment mechanisms. These sources with capital resources are equally frustrated with the performance limitations offered to them by conventional banks. The answer is to develop creative ways to link the source of capital directly with the small business and bypass conventional banking. This will be the beginning of an entirely new method of direct-lending that eliminates the bank middle-man and streamlines the entire process. The traditional "brick and mortar" bank will begin to fade into a more obscure financial servicing business.

* * *

Chapter 22

Designing a Logo to Establish Your Brand and Image

While you might be creative, it's best to leave this one to the professionals.

* * *

STIFF COMPETITION faces the businesses of today. Every marketer struggles to achieve or maintain success, despite these harsh conditions. Corporate logos are used as identities to serve the purpose of representing enterprises. A logo puts a businessperson in a position where s/he is able to distinguish the image of the business from its opponents. Therefore, it goes on to play a crucial role in marketing the brand name of the business.

There exists a large number of techniques when designing a corporate logo. The Internet gives a range of templates and can contribute a great deal in helping the marketer come up with an attractive trademark for the organization. Another logo creation option is hiring logo experts to do it for the organization. The experts work on a variety of formats to create a logo that is impressive and satisfies the organization's desire. This is achieved through a healthy interaction between the logo professionals and the client—the marketing wing of the organization. This way, the relationship fosters a defined understanding of the organization's nature.

Also, it is essential to be aware of the philosophies governing and guiding the organization. With this knowledge, the logo design professionals can add a commendable definition to the organization's graphic symbol; they have the skills to add a deeper meaning to the brand name of the organization. These services present a client with an ability to review multiple forms of the graphic symbol. Reliable services permit a marketer to make necessary revisions of the trade mark if s/he happens to be dissatisfied. The panel of specialists also goes through systematic and detailed analysis for organizing an ideal and suitable graphic mark for an organization. A perfectly designed logo allows a bystander to ascertain the brand of an organization. All of the above is feasible during the designing of an impressive logo for the company.

An imperative aspect to remember is that logo designs are supposed to be simple and eye-catching. The most effective and recognizable logos use simple color patterns and a readable text. It's counter-productive and unprofessional to come up with an unnecessarily flamboyant logo. As discussed above, having a professional design your logo is a prudent investment since the designers have the skills and training to create a logo that will suit your company. Again, it is necessary for the company logo to be innovative and dissimilar to any other logo of a different company.

Lastly, when designing a logo, a company should be on the lookout not to embrace heavy decorations with diverse combinations of colors in the design. The primary element in a logo design is for it to be able to convey the nature of the product to the client, not give them a headache!

* * *

Chapter 23

The Importance of Domain Names

If no one searches for your business or business' name, how would they find your website?

* * *

MOST INDIVIDUALS believe that it is important to purchase one or more domain names that either exactly match or capture most of their business' name. I don't disagree with this move. It is important to own the rights to your own business' matching URL. However, once it's in the company's possession, it's safe. Other than making sure to renew the domain, an individual or business won't have to worry about someone trying to build a website that plays off of the business' name and reputation, assuming that the individual or business has every intention of growing in size, scope, revenue, popularity and credibility.

Understand that one of the most important factors used by popular search engines to determine a website's relevancy is to compare the keyword phrases being submitted during a query to the keywords that make up a website's domain name or URL. In order to best accomplish this, think long and hard about what your target audience will be searching for on the web. If you are an accountant in the Chicago area and your firm is called "Tom's Bookkeeping," don't build a website using the domain name www.TomsBook keeping.com. The obvious reason being that if you want to acquire new customers via search engines, you will be disappointed by the simple fact that people who have never heard of Tom's Bookkeeping aren't going to be searching for "Tom's Bookkeeping." Instead, buy the domain name www.chicagolandaccounting.com (or something to that effect) and use that. Why? Because it's more likely that people in the Chicago area will make general queries for Chicago or Chicago Land Accounting.

Now, before you go out and think you are going to buy every domain name that consists of keywords or keyword phrases related to your business, product, service or industry, remember that registrants already hold most one and two word domain names. The idea of purchasing large volumes of domain names for future resale has been around for over a decade. Most keyword matching or closely matching domain names are probably taken. This doesn't mean you or your company can't purchase them; it simply means you may have to negotiate to purchase the desired domain name for a premium.

Don't worry; if you're thinking about whether or not to build a website with the business name domain or the product or industry specific URL, remember that you can always set up a permanent 301-redirect that forwards individuals from one domain to another, in the event that someone types in www.yourbusinessname.com. Just make sure that the domain name that you believe will capture more website traffic is the primary associate with your website.

* * *

Chapter 24

How to Patent a New Product

A step-by-step guide to getting your product patented.

* * *

TOO OFTEN, I hear about peoples' dreams of starting a business stagnated by government paperwork. They talk about how they have all these great plans to start a new business around a product or invention they have developed, but never get the endeavor off the ground because they're deterred by the paperwork. Here is a step-by-step guide to getting past the paperwork and on your way to building your new business.

1. First, you need to find out if your product has already been patented. You can accomplish this by running a simple search with the United States Patent and Trademark Office on their website, www.uspto.gov. If you discover that someone has already patented your idea, I'm sorry, I'm afraid that unless you think of a new way to use your product, there isn't much you can do.

2. If your product hasn't already been patented, your next step is to decide what type of patent for which you want to apply. There are three types: (1) Design Patents (for ornamental characteristics), (2) Plant Patents (for new varieties of asexually produced plants), or the most common (3) Utility Patents (for useful process, machine, article of manufacture, or composition of matter).

3. Once you decide which of the three types of patents fits your idea the best, you must determine a filing strategy. This

involves answering the question whether you want to file in the United States only, or if you want International Protection. International Protection involves international cooperation among various worldwide Intellectual Property Offices.

4.   Assuming that you want to file a Utility Patent, which is the most common type, you will need to decide if you want to file a Provisional or Non-provisional Application. Don't be scared by the long words; basically, Provisional is an informal filing, while Non-provisional is a formal (and much more tedious process). While the Provisional process is easier, I would recommend taking the time and effort, if possible, to protect your idea right by completing the Non-provisional Application process.

5.   The fifth step is optional. It is expedited examination. The U.S. Patent and Trademark Office (USPTO) offers an Accelerated Examination Program where, basically, if you meet certain qualifications, you can "jump the line" and get your patent processed faster.

6.   Now, you're ready to make the final decision before filing: who will do the actual filing? Will you file yourself (pro se) or use a registered attorney or agent? While many people undertake the process of filing themselves, it is recommended that you use an attorney or agent to complete the actual filing. This will ensure that your application not be returned or delayed for inadequate completion. This is a perfect example of having to spend a little money to make money, but it's definitely worth it in the long run.

7.   Next, you'll prepare for electronic filing. Here, you'll determine your application processing fees and apply for a customer number and digital certificate. You can determine your application fees and apply for your customer number and digital certificate directly on the USPTO website. Your customer number allows you to easily manage all of your filings and correspondence with the USPTO and your digital certificate is a security measure that will uniquely identify you and allow you secure access to your patent information and data.

8. Now it's time to apply for your patent. I recommend that you use the USPTO's Electronic Filing System (EFS) as a registered eFiler. Using the EFS, anyone with an Internet connection can file patent applications and documents without downloading special software or changing document preparation tools and processes.

9. The good news about the ninth step is that you don't have to do anything! After you (or your attorney or agent) have completed the eighth step and submitted your application, the ninth step involves the USPTO examining your application. You can check your application status at any point on the website, using your Customer Number and Digital Certificate from Step 7. At the end of this step, if the USPTO gives you a "thumbs up" and your application is accepted, congratulations! Jump down to Step 12!

10. If the USPTO doesn't accept your application on the first try, no big deal. Don't get discouraged. You have several options here. You can file replies, requests for reconsideration, and appeals as necessary.

11. This step is another one that you need not take any action. Step 11 is the USPTO's reply to your request or appeal from Step 10. If, after your appeal or request, the USPTO decides to overturn their rejection and accepts your application, they will send you a Notice of Allowance and any due fees that you may owe from their additional attention.

12. The good news, if you've made it to this point in the patent filing process, is that your patent has been accepted and only one small step stands in your way before your patent is granted! The bad news is that now, you have to pay the issue and publication fees. Once the USPTO processes your payment, the patent is granted and your product is protected.

13. One final step involves the preservation of your protection. Maintenance fees are due 3 1/2, 7 1/2, and 11 1/2 years after the initial patent is granted.

In closing, the United States Patent and Trademark Office has done an exceptional job streamlining their electronic filing and informational system. In the United States, patenting through the USPTO is the only recognized option, but they make it easy and affordable. To learn more, see their website at www.uspto.gov.

* * *

Chapter 25

The Difference Between Copyrights & Trademarks

Ensure that you're protecting your intellectual property the right way.

* * *

PROTECTION OF INTELLECTUAL property is very important, especially if you're building a new business around it. Below is a list of "Fun Facts" that you may not have known about these similar, but legally different, protection practices.

A copyright, by definition, is a set of exclusive rights granted by a state to the creator of an original work or their assignee for a limited period of time upon disclosure of the work. This includes the right to copy, distribute and adapt the work.

A trademark (trade mark or trade-mark), by definition, is a distinctive sign or indicator used by an individual, business organization, or other legal entity to identify that the products or services to consumers with which the trademark appears originate from a unique source, and to distinguish its products or services from those of other entities.

© is the copyright symbol in a copyright notice.

™ is the symbol for an unregistered trademark (a mark to promote a brand or goods).

SM is the symbol for an unregistered service mark (a mark to promote or brand services).

® is the symbol for a registered trademark.

A copyright is obtained through the United States Copyright Office (USCO), which is a division of the Library of Congress.

A trademark is obtained through the United States Patent and Trademark Office (USPTO).

A copyright protects works of authorship as fixed in a tangible form of expression. Examples of what a copyright covers include works of art, photos, pictures, graphic designs, drawings, songs, music and sound recordings of all kinds, books, manuscripts, publications and other written works, plays, software, movies, shows, and other performance arts.

If you are interested in protecting a title, slogan, or other short word phrase, generally, you want a trademark.

Keep in mind that there may be occasions when both copyright and trademark protection are desired for the same project. For example, a marketing campaign for a new product may introduce a new slogan for use with the product, which also appears in advertisements for the product. Copyright and trademark protection will cover different things. The advertisement's text and graphics, as published, will be covered by copyright. This will not, however, protect the slogan. The slogan may be protected by trademark law, but this will not cover the rest of the advertisement. If you want both forms of protection, you will have to perform both types of registration with the United States Trademark and Patent Office (www.uspto.gov) and the United States Copyright Office (www.copyright.gov).

Initially, copyright law applied only to the copying of books.

Blacksmiths who made swords in the Roman Empire are thought of as being the first users of trademarks.

This has been a basic collection of "fun facts" surrounding copyrighting and trademarking in the United States. The websites of the respective offices of control listed above offer a wealth of further information, tutorials, step-by-step walk-throughs, and other valuable information that can get you on your way to protecting your intellectual property.

The bottom line is that protection of your intellectual property should be your very first step when starting a new business or project that depends on your intellectual property. Also, just because you've conjured up a great concept or idea doesn't mean that you're the first to come up with it. Due yourself a favor before you start marketing your new idea and check with the before mentioned government offices in order to ensure that you're not accidentally taking credit for something someone else has already registered or copyrighted.

* * *

Chapter 26

The Name's Bond, Surety Bond

You might be licensed and insured, but are you bonded?

* * *

OCCASIONALLY, a small business, especially those performing contracting services, will be asked to bond their work in advance. In some states, certain types of contractors are required to be bonded.

If you live and work in the following states, you may need to be commercially bonded: Alabama, Colorado, Connecticut, Delaware, Washington D.C., Florida, Indiana, Kentucky, Louisiana, Maryland, Massachusetts, Minnesota, Mississippi, Missouri, Nevada, New Hampshire, New Jersey, New York, North Carolina, Ohio, Oklahoma, Pennsylvania, Rhode Island, South Carolina, Tennessee, Texas, Utah, Virginia, West Virginia, and Wisconsin.

While the following states do not require bonding, they do require pre-opening escrow: Georgia, Hawaii, Illinois, Iowa, Oregon, and Washington (state).

Simply put, a bond is a financial guarantee that you will honor a business contract. Sometimes referred to as a "surety bond," a bond is a third party obligation promising to pay if a vendor does not fulfill its valid obligations under a contract. There are various types of bonds such as LICENSE bond, PERFORMANCE bond, BID bond, INDEMNITY bond, and PAYMENT bond make up the different types of bonds.

- A LICENSE bond is required by some states for certain businesses. In some cases, you pay the state directly rather than obtaining a bond.

- A PERFORMANCE bond is a guarantee that you will perform work in accordance with the terms of a contract.

- A BID bond is a guarantee you will perform work if the bid is won by you.

- An INDEMNITY bond promises to reimburse losses incurred if you fail to perform or if you fail to pay other vendors in the performance of the contact.

- A PAYMENT bond promises that you will pay all subcontractors and material providers utilized in the performance of a contract.

It is important to remember that a bond is *not* an insurance policy. A bond only provides assurance that the contracted work will be satisfactorily completed. For example, your bond will not pay for property damage or personal injury resulting from your work. For this, you need conventional insurance coverage.

A simple Google search will list companies that provide bonding services under "surety bonds" in your area. In general, bonding companies will only provide bond coverage in an amount that you can cover with existing liquid assets.

Before you purchase a bond from any bonding company, have the bond documentation reviewed by your attorney and ensure that you understand exactly what the bond can and cannot protect against. This will benefit both you and your customer.

* * *

Chapter 27

Greatest Startup Challenges

Regardless of the industry, these are the most common challenges. Start preparing for them now.

* * *

WHILE STARTING A BUSINESS is always, in a word, well, *challenging*, there are a few common challenges that we see travel across the entire spectrum of starting a business, in virtually every type of startup, regardless of the field or medium. By identifying these common challenges, you can plan for them ahead of time, hopefully coasting over them like speed bumps when they arrive, not crashing into them like an invisible mountain in the fog.

Most commonly, when you are in the very early stages of starting a business, you will find that you act as every single employee and thus, have every single job to do. In short, you have to do everything yourself; from balancing the books to the creative design, from coming up with an initial marketing initiative to seeking out sources of funding. These areas may not always be your strongest, so be prepared to ask for help.

When starting a new business, time is always of the essence because time is money. Not just making it, but also spending it. As such, be prepared to learn a lot of new things, and learn them *quickly*. The quicker you learn, the faster your growth will be, and the faster your first real paycheck will arrive. As most salty entrepreneurs have come to realize, most things never go as planned. In business, you are constantly affected by outside sources—customers, consultants, the weather, etc. The bad news is that you typically can't control any of those things, so keeping your cash flow under control is huge. Before you even get your first customer, you'll have to purchase supplies, incur government paperwork fees, initial marketing and logo design, etc. Be ready for these things and don't be shocked if you have to pay a few bills before your first customer arrives.

While I've mentioned it briefly, this next point deserved as much clarity as I can muster: time management. I'll say it again: time management. When you're starting a small business, time management is everything. It is the foundation of everything. Without good time management, you can't possibly do everything yourself, you will inevitably learn everything slowly, and your cash flow will fly out the window faster than a frightened parakeet on speed. Compartmentalize your tasks and don't be a scatter-brain. Finish a project before you move on to the next one. The only appropriate deviation from this plan is if you rely on outside resources and you have to pause a plan in the middle to wait for someone else's addition, whether it be a design conversion, a lawyer's signature, etc., before you can continue.

Finally, stay focused and maintain balance. Once you've compartmentalized—prioritize! Don't waste your time going to buy excess pens when you have a deadline pending or you can't launch a new product until you think of a name or finish the design! When you're starting a business, your greatest priority is to finish the revenue-bearing projects first. The only time that you should chase that goal directly is if you have to temporarily deviate to pursue action that will achieve your goal of bringing in the revenue better and/or faster.

* * *

Part IV

Stayin' Alive

Chapter 28

The State of the Small Biz

Chances are, if you bought this book, you either currently own, or desire to own, a small business. The way forward begins here.

* * *

The Reality…

The arena of small business is transforming with real-time change like never before. Complex new strategies and trends are rapidly reshaping the way business is transacted. These changes have influenced the way service is provided and the method in which products are marketed and sold. Many believe the small business owner has entered a new era where the knowledge and implementation of these trends is crucial to the future success of their enterprise. Others merely view today's market as ultra-competitive. The reality is that both views are accurate. The important question is which description is applicable for the business? Often, for the necessity of regaining a competitive edge, or in some instances for the sheer sake of survival, wholesale change is eminent. However, for the majority of businesses, the solution is quite simple: improve upon the current path, but with a fresh perspective.

The Challenges….

The physician is easily the most well-known in the area and the best at what he does. The construction company has the most skilled laborers and has been in business longer than any of its competition. The interior designer has the largest clientele and has won the most awards. *"But where are the referrals?" "Why are sales down this quarter?" "Why is the business not forging new ground?"* **A dilemma commences.**

The aforementioned questions are not simply random in nature; they are the concern of every business owner at some point. In fact, small and large businesses alike are in constant pursuit of the next big thing that will distinguish them from others. Total disregard of these concerns directly places the ultimate outcome of success in the balance and will in no way meet the desired goals. As a result, new issues arise: Does the business in question expand or does it downsize? Does it relocate, cut costs, or spend more to reach its targets? Is additional advertising or promotion of the product or service the answer? *"Am I qualified to answer these critical questions with my business as collateral?" "Where do I begin?"*

The Way Forward…

Understanding in which direction to proceed always requires a review of the past. Knowing this, a historical review of traditional methods reveals that sales, customer service, and the bottom line were always the initial focal points cited by independent businesses as key elements in maintaining profitability and market share. While these elements remain critical to success, the reality for the business owner of today is much more intricate and ever-changing. **Welcome to the way forward.**

Image, market presence, diversity, technology, innovation and non-traditional approaches are now the buzz. To maximize the scope and to encompass all facets of the business framework, the utilization of existing resources for entrepreneurs and businesses seeking answers, advice and direction for success in the marketplace, can assist in understanding and employing the components critical to a business' success. The future demands that every prosperous enterprise amplify its energies beyond just the core fundamentals to become a leader in its category. *"How does this work for my small business?"*

The way forward begins here…

* * *

Chapter 29

The Importance of Legal and Accounting Representation

Don't mistake these important expenses for things that belong in your "unnecessary costs" pile.

* * *

IN ORDER TO CREATE a business that will thrive through all the fluctuations in the industry, you will need extraordinary planning as well as exceptional analysis. You will also need to make continuous decisions that will not harm the business. Therefore, the success or the failure of the business will largely depend on your business acumen. Second to that will be the quality of your services or products. There are some business basics that you should keep in mind when you are starting a business. One of the most important (and most commonly overlooked) is the legal and accounting representation of the business.

When you start developing your business, the first thing that you will need to entrench is both your accounting and legal roles. Very small businesses that tend to be owned by a sole proprietor or run by a partnership can realistically perform their own accounting and their bookkeeping. Similarly, for legal representation, the very small business can also contract a personal lawyer who will look into things when the need arises. However, for companies with a much larger structure, this has to be handled differently. Larger companies will need to employ an accountant for their accounting representation. Depending on how big the company is, the business may even need to enlist the help of banking professionals for their accounting needs.

The same applies for the legal representation of a large business. Larger companies are better off contracting a law firm to handle their legal representation, as a personal lawyer would find the workload overwhelming. Before you sign a contract with anyone to do either your accounting or legal representation, ensure that you have done the proper background check and performance research. This does not matter whether it is a small business or a large company as the ramifications would be the same if you trusted your business to an individual or a firm that is unscrupulous or incompetent. Getting the right legal and accounting representation for your company will ensure that it will not suffer any unnecessary downfalls or losses.

Accounting representation for your business is also important as it enables you to accurately assess the financial performance of your business. Documents such as financial statements, cash flow statements, and even balance sheets give you an indication of how well your business is doing or if you are incurring losses. This, in turn, enables you to plan a way forward if the business is making losses. Without accounting representation, you will not have an idea of where your business is headed because you will not be able to accurately take into account any revenues or profits that your business has made.

One major mistake that most businesses make when they begin to become successful is that they forget the importance of legal representation as well as accounting representation. Instead, they focus on customer service, which should not be neglected, but neither should the financial and legal part of the business. Getting accurate legal and accounting representation could make or break a business.

* * *

Chapter 30

How to Write a Press Release

Use these proven ideas when developing effective press releases and impress your target audiences while achieving SEO success.

* * *

- This first one is basic—use your business logo whenever possible and don't miss out on an opportunity to build brand recognition. Make sure that your business' logo is on all of its press releases, preferably near at the top, so the viewers don't miss seeing it.

- Ensure that the press release includes real news. The press release needs to draw positive attention to your business.

- Be cognizant of where the key elements of your message are located in the press release. The main point of the press release should be included in the headline, subheading and in the first paragraph. Most viewers only read the first couple of paragraphs of press releases and for search engine indexing purposes, remember that the most relevant content should be in the beginning of the press release.

- Create a specific headline, typically not more than 20 words, that includes a clear and to-the-point message about the press release. Remember that search engines and other types of software and crawler programs can't usually read any hidden meanings, puns or marketing slogans, therefore clean and understandable headlines perform best when trying to maximize the popularity and ranking of the press release. Just remember, some people are more inclined to read further into catchy headlines. This isn't a catch-22, but be sure to use reason and logic when creating a headline to enhance the potential viewing audience.

Another valuable component of a press release is the sub-headline. Subheads offer the press release creator the ability to provide additional information to viewers when they are deciding if they want to continue reading the press release. Also, in regard to search engine optimization or "SEO," this is a wonderful spot to include keywords and keyword phrases that may have been left out of the primary headline.

- Provide links in the beginning of the press release and continue to include them frequently. Appropriate links, in the form of anchor-text and hyperlinks, assist search engines as they index the press release by associating the content of the press release with other related content sources and sites. This strategy provides additional context to readers of the press release. Always link the first mention of a brand or product name that is being discussed to the appropriate landing page on the business' website. Also, be sure to create links for the names in a press release to individual biographies or the person's social media profile page(s).

- Probably something that doesn't need to be mentioned, but just in case, be sure to provide accurate contact information. Don't get caught in a situation where numerous people or businesses want to contact your organization but you forgot to include it or you never changed the information after the company changed addresses, phone numbers, or points of contact. Seriously, it happens. Ensure that your readers have the necessary information to contact your business. This includes point of contact, address, phone number(s), fax number, emails, social media links, website, and any other means of communication that you have available for individuals or business to reach you.

- Don't forget to format. Not unlike other media outlets, the presentation of the information is crucial. Be sure to use things like underlining, bullets, and bold or italic font to help convey any and all important parts of the press release. If the press release is standard font and includes limited formatting, separate content so the reader can move through the press release in manageable pieces. Remember college textbooks? Same concept. Make key words and phrases stand out so that busy readers or those who don't have a lot of time can still understand the message, even with limited exposure.

- This doesn't apply to most; however, in the event that the business is publicly traded, provide the specific exchange, the company's ticker or stock symbol, and its International Securities Identifier Number. By including these pieces of information, the press release will become easier to find in a multitude of news networks and databases.

As a final note—use multimedia. Whether it is a reader, consumer or journalist, most people prefer to look at something with supporting media, such as pictures, videos or audio clips. Studies have shown that press releases with multimedia are more likely to be viewed.

* * *

Chapter 31

Small Business Tax Tips

Taxes can be a cinch if addressed right, or a nightmare if addressed wrong. Here are some tips to keep your business ready for April 15th at all times.

* * *

TO EFFECTIVELY manage a new business, you need to know how to effectively file the business' taxes. All business owners are expected to file taxes at one point or another throughout the year. It doesn't matter whether you are making a profit or reporting losses. While most people find this process quite daunting, it doesn't have to be that way. All you really need to ensure is that you have the appropriate tools to aid you in the process, as well as the appropriate people. The following tips should make filing taxes a bit easier for any small business owner.

The first thing you need to do is to ensure that someone with impeccable bookkeeping skills is keeping track of things for your business. Now is not the time to be overzealous; if you can't do it properly yourself, hire someone who can. Most business owners find bookkeeping quite intimidating. If you are feeling overwhelmed and have no idea how to go about it, we highly suggest that you hire a professional to do it for you. If you're on the fence, keep in mind that sourcing out this task isn't nearly as daunting as being audited by the IRS. Although you will be paying an accountant or bookkeeper, at least you can be guaranteed that you are not making losses due to poor accountability of finances. If the business' bookkeeping is done shoddily, it will be reflected in the financial statements. This will make it even more difficult to file the business' taxes.

Like attorneys or real estate agents, a bookkeeper does not have to be hired as a permanent employee. Small businesses can get good bookkeepers once a month for several hours or a couple of days, depending on how much work needs to be done. Most short-term bookkeepers charge on hourly basis. After they are done putting the books in order, you can choose to either let them file your tax returns for you, or you can do this on your own. If you let them do it for you, they will have to keep the records so that they can take them to the IRS on your behalf.

Another thing you can do to keep your tax filing hassle-free is to have all the documents pertaining to your business in order before you file. Filing taxes for small businesses requires one to be meticulous. If any of the miscellaneous documents is missing, the process can be dragged out for months. You need to establish a filing system from the very start of your business so that you can have all the necessary paperwork in order. Just because it is a filing system for a business doesn't mean that it has to be complicated. Make it as simple and as logical as you can so that you can easily track whatever paperwork you may need for the process.

Another convenient way to ensure that your tax filing is hassle-free is to file your taxes with the use of online software. The great thing about this is that your business' tax information will be stored on the server for several years so you can always double check it whenever you want to.

* * *

Chapter 32

How to Set Yourself Apart in the Market

Got a degree in general business? So do the other 50 applicants. Here's how to get the job.

* * *

TODAY, THERE ARE MULTITUDES of people out there seeking jobs without any major or formal area of specialization. Sure, they have a general business degree, but no area of specialization in business or specialized training of any kind. If you're just starting a new business, instead of applying for a job at someone else's, this is important to you, too, so that you can put yourself in the shoes of people who will eventually apply for a position at your organization and pick out the stellar candidates, not just the ones with the heaviest resumes or most prestigious alma maters.

As an applicant, remember that summer internship you turned down so you could wander around Europe for a month with your friends before you joined the "workforce"? Well, you probably should have taken it, because right now, you and your general business degree look exactly like the twenty other people sitting there with their general business degrees waiting to go into your interviews. C'est la vie. Do yourself (and your career) a favor and bulk up your reputability with a minor or even a second major in something specialized like marketing, finance, management, writing, or something that will enhance your education and set you apart from the masses of other "general business" applicants.

There are several areas of specialization in business. One of these areas is the marketing field. This is a very popular business field in which many people have invested additional time. One can make themselves marketable (no pun intended) in this field by taking other courses apart from the general business degree. These courses include marketing strategy, business development, Internet marketing, etc. A minor in something like marketing will ice the cake of your career. You will be set to go out there and market yourself as a businessperson with marketing knowledge and experience. Make yourself a two-for-one deal!

These courses can also be good in assisting one looking to start their own business. The ability of having marketing skills enables one to have the foresight and ability to connect with customers. This will also reduce the expense of hiring experts to give you marketing tips or substitute the expense of getting business consultants.

If you've already joined the workforce and want to make yourself more promotable or secure during downsize time, it's never been easier or more affordable to go back to school via online universities. In fact, your company might even have scholarship opportunities or a student loan repayment program. By knocking out one or two courses at a time at night, you will make yourself much more valuable to your company, and yourself, because, aside from the additional credentials, you *will* be learning new skills that you can apply around the office.

Finally, your resume or curriculum vitae is a detailed document which involves both professional and co-curricular activities. It should include everything you think can assist you in getting the job or promotion you want. Most people tend to forget any professional or technical certifications they might have, aside from their formal education. Some of these certifications are the ones that can make you stand out from a crowd of professionals or new applicants with the same educational qualifications as you. It is also good to include any seminars you attend in your professional career. Include the date when you attended the seminars and when the certificate was issued and the organization that issued it.

* * *

Chapter 33

Trust Over Talent

Jumping ship will only cause your career to sink. Here's why.

* * *

NOWADAYS, BUSINESSES, especially small business, are just trying to stay afloat. They are trying to keep their doors open by supplying their customers with the best products and services available. More often than not, a superior staff will produce a superior product. The staff with the most talent, the most (or best) education, and the most experience will deliver the best product. The delta that most business owners have to settle on, however, is how to get the best products or services out of the best staff member that he or she can afford to employ.

Beyond the quality and talent of the staff, a more important facet has emerged: loyalty. Business owners have found that a company filled with new people (regardless of talent) will not perform as well as a team that has worked together on multiple projects for an extended period of time. As such, during an employment interview, the intent of the employee can often weigh more on the business owner's decision to hire them than their credentials. The reason is this: it is not uncommon for businesses to operate on projects beyond the scope of typical education. In short, what you learned in high school and/or college might not have anything to do with what the company or position for which you are applying is currently working on.

This fact, combined with the fact that it costs the company a lot of time and money to train someone and get them up to speed on a project or position, means that someone applying for a position may or may not get the job if they seem unsure about how long they would like to stay with the organization with which they are applying.

Think about it: why would you hire someone if they seemed like they were going to jump ship at the next slightly better offer that came their way; or if it seems like they are just bringing in a paycheck from you until their real "dream job" comes along.

I have a friend who graduated at the top of his class and is an extremely talented graphic designer—about as good as I've ever seen. The guy's a visionary. However, he recently expressed to me that he is having trouble getting somebody to hire him. Having seen his work, I couldn't believe it. I asked him about his employment history after college and his answer clarified his situation to me.

My friend was basically recruited out of college by a big design firm at a respectable starting salary. Not long after he settled into his first company, he was extended an offer slightly better by a different company, so he went for it. Not long after that, he was offered something slightly better from a third, so he went for it. After four companies in fewer than three years, the economy took a dip and because he was the "new guy" at his newest company, he got the ax first. He was labeled disloyal by his industry and had trouble finding employment because, now having to interview, his new potential employers wanted to know why he had had so many jobs in such a short amount of time. It might have even been better for him if he was laid off from those jobs because at least he would still have the trust of the business owners in his industry.

This is why interviewers ask about your "five-year professional plan," "where you see yourself in ten years," or "what your dream job is." They are looking for loyalty; someone who wants to be rooted with them for a long time as because previously discussed, it costs time and money to bring even the most talented new employee onto the team.

The moral: be smart and stick around for a while. You'll be better off in the long run. If you're in the process of starting your own business, when you get to the hiring process, now you know whom to look for and what to ask.

* * *

Chapter 34

The Worst Entrepreneurial Mistakes

(and how to avoid them)

Get right what so many others get wrong.

* * *

Thinking that you can do it all and accomplish your goals without help.

Just because you might be starting a business alone doesn't mean that you won't need help. Success depends on developing and using a network of colleagues, friends, mentors and professionals that can provide advice, assistance and direction in tough times. Two professional fields that I always recommend to friends or clients who are starting up a new business are lawyers and accountants. With the vast margin of error in the legal and bookkeeping arenas of business startup, they more than pay for themselves in preventative maintenance.

Thinking for one second that you don't need a business plan.

It's a true fact that there is a direct correlation between planning and success. By failing to plan, you are planning to fail. Some foolish entrepreneurs think that they can coast through the planning process and make adjustments to their plans as they go along. Others have the foolish misconception that a business plan would limit their creativity or spontaneity. Others still feel that their business isn't large enough or complex enough to warrant a plan. Here's the deal: every business can benefit from a business plan, no matter what size it is. The process of developing a business plan organizes your strategy and helps you chart your priorities.

Assuming that you'll make it big quickly or easily.

I'll be honest with you; when you're starting a business, there's good news and bad news. The good news is that by starting a business, you'll get to live out your dreams; the bad news is that no matter what you do, it's never as easy as you think it will be. There are a lot of assumptions tied up with the practice of starting a business. The reality is that success takes very long hours, strategic planning, and a die-hard commitment to the legwork involved. While the end-result is wonderful once the work is done, the work is never as easy as you think it will be.

Not conducting a market test or doing research.

Just because you have a great idea doesn't mean you have a business. The most common question among would-be entrepreneurs after conceptualizing a new idea is, *now what*? Just because you've thought of a great concept or idea doesn't mean that the 'Great Idea Fairy' is going to visit you in the night and give you a million dollars. Patenting, trademarking or copyrighting your great idea is a good start—right before you start writing your business plan.

* * *

Part V

When Tomorrow Becomes Today

Chapter 35

Starting a Web-Based Business

(An overview)

Don't make the mistake of thinking that your web-based business shouldn't be run like a storefront business. Without proper planning, you'll fail just as fast.

* * *

THERE ARE MANY STEPS to starting a web-based business or even adding an electronic component to your brick-and-mortar business—everything from building an e-commerce website, setting up merchant banking, and creating marketing, to developing the necessary wholesale distribution relationships. The first of the necessary steps is, naturally, to create the idea. This is the general business plan, deciding in what industry to get involved, and outlining how, and why, your model will work, compared to the competition.

During the development stage of the business planning process, it is important to flush out all ideas pertaining to the venture. Decide on potential clients, where to sell, how to market, and what to expect as it pertains to sales volume and revenue numbers. Remember to write out a business plan just as any other business, as well as calculating all logical contingencies.

After all general business knowledge has been laid out and plans have been put into place, it is time to build the necessary distribution relationships. The most common approach is to seek out a nationwide wholesaler and inquire about account possibilities. Most often, this level of distributorship costs a small fee and yields emerging businesses with very competitive bottom lines.

When nearing the end of this segment of development, it is a good idea to get started on the e-commerce website. The website should be very easy to navigate and provide readers with the most up-to-date information regarding the industry and products offered. Don't be fooled! This takes time and patience. Many websites out there offer only a small variety of products and have minimal information. It is important to spend the necessary amount of time developing this for your clients, especially if the web is going to be your primary medium of exposure.

The website should contain an extensive database of products that include recognizable titles, pictures, detailed descriptions and prices, if possible. Ensure to list your business on eBay, Amazon and other e-commerce compilers. Also, create different forms of search queries that make referencing your product catalog easy.

Next, during the merchant phase, choose a service provider that has a great track-record. You don't want to get caught in a situation where transactions are not going through for reasons unknown to you or poor customer service. Look for reasonable monthly fees and nominal transaction costs that you feel are congruent with your business model. The easiest way to accomplish this is to study your competition. Make sure to accept e-checks and pay pal; surprisingly, these two forms of payment are very common in the online world. When setting up your online merchant banking, remember two important things: first, make sure you have security in place to temporarily hold unusual transactions, such as those coming from IP addresses foreign to the billing address or limited customer information. Second, allow yourself the ability to authorize virtual transactions via your personal computer or application. This makes doing business on the go or over the phone extremely convenient.

From there, develop your marketing. Build e-mailers that you can send to pre-paid list recipients or existing customers. Make sure there is plenty of fulfillment material. Most consumers respond to collateral sales material more than anything because it is coming from a trusted source. Think about industry events, blogs, chat rooms, and magazines.

Like a business with a brick-and-mortar (tangible) store-front, planning and research is key is the success of a web-based business. When writing a business plan, if you intend to acquire outside financing, ensure to stay on top of listing expenses exclusive to your web-based business like web-hosting fees, graphic design, and any other technology costs for hardware or software.

* * *

Chapter 36

Important Steps when Starting a Web-Based Business

(Into the weeds)

Like finely-tuned racecar, subtle website tweaks and adjustments can skyrocket popularity. Here's why.

* * *

DO YOU EVER wonder why websites change? Maybe it's the colors, the navigation icons, or content changes. Most changes that occur on websites are not random. They are typically very specific changes that the Webmaster or site owner has decided to make because of analytics and test results from a multitude of fronts.

When creating a web-based business, there are many different components that exist beyond most individuals' field of vision. Quite often, business owners or website creators attempt to conceptualize what they think is a perfect website without focusing on things like analytics, Internet marketing, social media, and search engine optimization (SEO). Without these ever-so-critical items being addressed, a website, no matter how well-built, will struggle to survive in a sea of websites and web pages that are making the necessary efforts to obtain site traffic and get exposure across multiple platforms. Below are a few tools commonly used and, best of all, are usually available for free.

An easy first step is implementing a very basic analytics program. This code can easily be placed on every site page throughout the entire website. Analytics are a must, due to the immeasurable value it offers site owners, developers or Webmasters.

With analytics properly installed on every page, then validated, these individuals can track visitors in multiple capacities such as number of page views, how long viewers stayed on the website, bounce rates, and other relevant metrics that are vital to the survival of a newly emerging website.

Another simple tactic used to maximize the effectiveness of a website is to set up a Webmaster tool to better track the metrics associated with your website. Webmaster programs are a must when tracking the metrics regarding your website. Be sure to look at things like crawl reports, indexed pages, and indexation issues, and also track basic statistics such as clicks, keywords and other traffic metrics. It is important to always be improving a website, to be sure that it is being ranked properly, and to make adjustments to enhance viewer retention.

Think of your website like a racecar; even if it looks great and sounds great, there is still some fine-tuning that can be done to achieve peak performance. With a little tweak here and a small adjustment there, while each doesn't seem like much, a handful of minute adjustments can easily produce noticeable results. Most adjustments are as easy as choosing one word over another and ensuring that you change little things every day. To the powers that make your website popular, changing one word everyday for 100 days is much better than changing 100 words in one day. While it's not quite that simple, that's the basic idea.

After an analytics program and a Webmaster tool have been addressed, it would be wise to run a crawl simulation. The purpose of a crawl simulation is to shed light on anything that was overlooked during the final phases of website development. Running a crawl simulation will bring most unknown errors, incomplete redirects, broken links, and missing titles to your attention, allowing for immediate changes. Every day that a site is live is, potentially, a day that it could be re-crawled by spiders; if this happens, you want to make sure that you have made the necessary changes to fix any existing mistakes, especially items mentioned above like improper redirects, broken links, files blocked by robot.txt and missing tags. These crawl simulations can be administered by *free* programs found on the web or they can be purchased tools. Either way you go, it is crucial to run a crawl simulation.

Once the crawl simulation is complete, it would be appropriate to test your website, more specifically—its design, with a browser emulator. Browser emulators are used to confirm that the design, layout and imagery work well and look great on multiple browsing platforms such as Safari, Internet Explorer, Firefox, Google Chrome, and anything else that you would like to check. This is also a great time to address any framing issues with mobile devices. We now live in an era of mobile devices, such as smart phones and tablets, so be sure that if you intend to be viewed on these devices, that your website is formatted properly to automatically frame to their screen sizes.

If your website is going to offer an RSS Feed (which it should), then you need to outfit your site with analytics to track the performance of the feed. There isn't too much mystery here besides believing that it is important to understand the metrics associated with your feed and making changes accordingly.

At some point, it is necessary to compile a list of contacts. This list should include everything from colleagues, business contacts, friends, and family. These individuals can be instrumental in building that much-needed buzz when launching a fresh, new website. Also, it would be wise to send out a few emails inviting your contacts to check out the site and give honest feedback. The communication can be created as a formal press release, a correspondence letter, or even a casual email with a lot of personal feel. I would recommend some kind of middle ground. Make sure it's not a pitch/sales email, but be sure to add a touch of pride and professionalism to your communication.

Essentially, there are many ways to properly plan, prep and monitor a website during every stage of its development. These few steps are extremely easy to implement and they can help not only webmasters, but website and business owners, in their quest to enhance and improve the quality of their website and its performance. Good luck, and hopefully you find some, if not all, of these tools useful in the continued evolution of your website.

* * *

Postface

Where to go from here?

IT MAY BE SAFE TO ASSUME that by reaching the end of this book, after reading the material provided, you are one of two types of individuals. The *curious* reader may have been interested in learning how a potentially successful business could be envisioned, created and then finally launched to compete in the marketplace. For *curious* readers, these pages may have even sparked some imagination in the thought process about becoming an entrepreneur one day. *Curious* readers have always shown interest in educating and informing themselves on a new topic and enhancing their knowledge-base while doing so.

The *serious* reader may have chosen to read our writings because he/she may have already decided to toss a hat in the ring and become an entrepreneur. Or perhaps, the business has been launched, and now having additional tools, expert guidance, and real-world examples to follow are vital for success. A serious reader never stops perusing every possible source for innovative ideas, the next greatest trend, or even a leg-up on their competition.

Curious or *serious*, it would be our hope that everyone who has read this first installment of our series found the material worthy of the read, and regardless of how or why you found us, we are glad you did.

For the guys who wrote this first installment, and also founded the Expert Business Advice website, the philosophy was simple:

- Create material of substance and value that can continue to be expanded indefinitely for the benefit of the reader, the customer, and the business professional

- Deliver the best possible idea, resources and guidance to those who seek it

- Take ownership of our work, stand by it, and be proud of it

Developing this material from several points of view; and delivering it to the masses from diverse backgrounds and from multiple levels of experience was crucial for us. In fact, it was the only way. Simply put, our goal with this series shares the same vision as our official slogan: "Experts Create | We Deliver | You Apply."

Coming soon in *The Crash Course Series*:

- *A Crash Course in Sales & Marketing*
- *A Crash Course in Business Management*
- *A Crash Course in Business Finance*
- *A Crash Course in the Legal Aspects of Business*

The way forward begins here…

www.ingramcontent.com/pod-product-compliance
Lightning Source LLC
Chambersburg PA
CBHW022111210326
41521CB00028B/293